AF423016

LAST DAYS OF PEKIN

PIERRE LOTI

Translated from the French by Myrta L. Jones

With a new preface by Claude Jaeck

Last Days of Pekin
Translated from the French by Myrta L. Jones

By Pierre Loti

ISBN-13: 978-988-8769-11-7

HISTORY / Asia / China

EB157

Published by Earnshaw Books Ltd. (Hong Kong)

PREFACE

Pierre Loti, one of the world's most prolific, romantic and exotic travel writers and novelists, was born as Julien Marie Viaud in Rochefort, western France in 1850. A childhood fascination with far-off lands across the ocean led him to embark on a naval career that enabled him to find adventure and love across the globe.

Loti's education began in his birthplace. At the age of seventeen, he entered the naval school in Brest and studied at Le Borda. He gradually rose to the rank of captain in 1906. He drew on his real-life ocean-going experiences when writing the romantic novels and travel books that made him one of the most popular authors of his day. Although his prolific output brought him both fame and fortune, he remained a romantic escapist and never gave up his beloved naval career.

During the autumn of 1900, he went to China as part of the international expedition sent to combat the Boxer Rebellion. He described what he saw there after the siege of Peking. The Boxer Rebellion, also called the Boxer Uprising, took place between 1898 and 1901 and was a violent expression of opposition to imperialism and Christianity. The uprising took place in response to the creation of foreign "spheres of influence" in China with grievances ranging from the opium trade, political invasion, economic manipulation, and missionary evangelism. In China, popular sentiment was largely resistant to foreign influences and anger was high over the "unequal treaties" which the weak Qing state was unable to resist. Concern grew that missionaries and Chinese Christians could use the resultant decline to their advantage by appropriating the land and property of Chinese peasants to give to the church, even though they might be unwilling to do so. This sentiment resulted in violent revolts against foreign interests.

In June 1900 in Peking, Boxer fighters threatened foreigners, which forced them to seek refuge in the Legation Quarter of the city. In response, the initially hesitant Empress Dowager Cixi, urged by the conservatives of the Imperial Court, supported the Boxers and declared war on the foreign powers. Diplomats, foreign civilians and soldiers as well as Chinese Christians in the Legation Quarter were besieged by the Imperial Army and the Boxers for 55 days before being liberated.

During the siege, the Qing government equivocated between destroying the foreigners in the Legation Quarter and extending olive branches. Clashes were reported between different palace factions, those favouring war and those favouring conciliation, the latter led by Prince Qing. The supreme commander of the Chinese forces, Ronglu, claimed three years later that he acted to protect the besieged foreigners. The siege was raised when an Eight-Nation Alliance brought 20,000 armed troops to China, defeated the Imperial Army, and captured Peking. The Boxer Protocol of 7 September 1901 ended the uprising and imposed severe punishments including an indemnity of 67 million pounds.

No other French writer shared Pierre Loti's good fortune of arriving in China at the aftermath of the Boxer Rebellion, the one time in history when the Empire lay completely at the mercy of the colonial powers. Not only did Loti visit the private quarters of the Emperor and Empress Dowager in the Forbidden City, but he himself stayed in a palace inside the Imperial city.

Les Derniers Jours de Pekin chronicles Loti's activities in China from his arrival on board the battleship *Le Redoutable* in the Gulf of Pechili (24 September 1900) to the last night he spent in the Imperial city (4 May 1901). As aide-de-camp to Vice Admiral Pottier, he was sent ashore on two separate occasions, first to carry dispatches to the French Legation in Peking and later to represent Pottier at the funeral of a German officer who perished in an accidental fire.

His accounts of these two visits to the capital, first appeared in the newspaper *Le Figaro* and were later published as *Les Derniers Jours de Pekin* in 1902. By that time, the 50-year-old Captain of the French Navy was already well established as a writer of widely exotic novels and a member of the French Academy. His literary reputation served him well in a country where men of letters were greatly respected entitling him to a lavish reception from Chinese dignitaries, and even securing him an interview with the great statesman, Li Hongzhang.

As an officer with the French force, he was free to move in and out of the City, to visit palaces, temples, and Imperial mausoleums normally out of bounds to foreigners and ordinary Chinese citizens. Loti was thus in an unprecedented position to convey a great deal of new information to his readers back home.

His description of city street life, sceneries, costumes, food, music, acrobatics and architecture are in general lively and interesting. "… for us, barbarians, who are not initiated, the mystery of this palace is present in these three halls that are absolutely identical, with the same throne, the same carpet, the same ornaments in identical positions; they follow one another along the same line, always on the same precise axis of the four-walled cities, which together form the city of Peking; they follow one upon the other preceded by great marble courts and built upon the very same marbles terraces: one reaches them by way of identical stairs, identical imperial paths… But why three halls, seeing that one necessarily has to hide the other two and that it is necessary in order to go from the first to the second and from the second to the third, to descend each time to the bottom of a vast, mournful and viewless court, and climb back down only to re-ascend amidst masses of ivory colored marble, superb, but so monotonous and oppressive? There has to be some mysterious reason tied to the number three..." (Extract of *The Last Days of Pekin*)

Being an expert anthropologist, Loti intuits that he cannot understand the Forbidden City by looking at it through the eyes of a Westerner. With great sensibility, he is able to register strong impressions, but it results for him only in a sense of disorientation, almost frustration. His minute attention towards the buildings and to the decorations dismays him with the repetition of the elements and of the forms. They do not allow him to formulate a fundamental sense of Chinese architecture: the great importance given to empty spaces as an element of introduction and the valuation of "fabrication", and the counter position which proposes the interaction among opposites, cyclic repetition, the sense of flow that is within the eternally present yin-yang system, the conceptual basis of Chinese thought.

Throughout his work, Loti's prose never loses that customary music and evocative power which made him at one time a favorite author of Marcel Proust. And although *Les Derniers Jours de Pekin* is still marred by the maudlin sentimentality that makes Loti so outdated to modern readers, the book presents a compassionate view of China under foreign occupation following the Boxer Rebellion, even though he experiences so acutely the feelings of strangeness and disorientation in a dominated foreign land.

The book seems to fluctuate perpetually between two opposing trends which have characterized Europe's view of China over several centuries, ranging from the 'sinophilic' to the 'sinophobic'. Passages which 'humanize' the Chinese and present them as victims of both the fanatic Boxers and the foreign invaders are counterbalanced not only by vivid descriptions of Boxer atrocities but also by statements alleging the innate cruelty of the Chinese race.

Loti's admiration for the Chinese is almost exclusively based on his appreciation of their art. It is clear that the most satisfactory part of his experience in China was his exposure to Chinese art, much of which had never before been seen by Europeans.

Something good has therefore resulted from Europe's sacrilegious intrusion into the Chinese world. Visitors to Peking could never have imagined the splendor concealed within the city.

"Before leaving, I wanted once more to see the "Purple City", and the royal halls, this time entering, not by way of hidden passages and secondary doors... none of which our Western capitals were conceived with such uniformity and audacity. One can understand why the sight of Paris, the Louvres or Versailles did not excessively dazzle Chinese Ambassadors who came to Europe... The impression we have retained of huge dark temples, of vast yellow enamel roofs crowning the titanic enormity of the marble terraces, is almost transformed into helpless admiration, respect and awe." (Extract - *The Last Days of Pekin*)

Unfortunately, during the Boxer Rebellion, hundreds of these magnificently carved facades, the product of incalculable hours of human labor, were burned each day.

Les Derniers Jours de Pekin concludes on a melancholic note, as Loti and his friend Colonel Marchand stroll about the palace grounds after the ball. They are overcome by a feeling more poignant than the mild depression one often experiences after a long-awaited event is over. What will be the fate of the Chinese Empire? "It seems to us that this evening has just confirmed beyond a doubt the crumbling of Peking, that is to say the crumbling of the world." Even if the Chinese court were to return to the capital, he says, "Peking is finished, its prestige fallen, its mystery pierced".

Loti laments the passing of the old era. Upon his second visit to Peking in the spring of 1901, he feels that traditional China is irrevocably lost.

The concluding sentence of the book makes his view clear: "Nevertheless, this Imperial City was one of the last refuges for the unknown and the magical on earth, one of the last boulevards of very old humanity, incomprehensible for us and almost somewhat mystical."

The West needs to dream about China, not to understand it.

Claude R. JAECK
Honorary President, Societe d'Histoire des Francais de Chine
Honorary General Delegate for China, Le Souvenir Francais
October 2021

THE
LAST DAYS OF PEKIN

Translated from the French of
Pierre Loti

By

MYRTA L. JONES

Illustrated from Photographs, and Drawings
by Jessie B. Janes

ADMIRAL

The notes which I sent to the "Figaro" from China are to be collected in a volume which will be published in Paris before my return, so that it will be impossible for me to look it over. I am therefore a little uneasy as to how such a collection may turn out; it will doubtless contain much repetition. Yet I beg that you will accept this dedication as a token of the profound and affectionate respect of your first aide-de-camp. You will be more indulgent than any one else, because you know under what conditions it was written, — from day to day during a painful campaign in the midst of the continual excitement of life aboard ship.

I have restricted myself to noting the things which have come under my own observation while undertaking the missions to which you assigned me, and in the course of the journey which you allowed me to take into a certain part of China hitherto almost unknown.

When we reached the Yellow Sea, Pekin had been taken, and the war was over. I could, therefore, only observe our soldiers during the period of peaceful occupation. Under these circumstances I have seen them always kind and almost fraternal in manner toward the humblest of the Chinese. May my book contribute its small part toward destroying the shameful stories published against them!

Perhaps you may reproach me, Admiral, for saying almost nothing of the sailors who remained on our ships, who were constantly toiling with never a murmur or a loss of courage

during our long and dangerous sojourn in the waters of
Petchili. Poor sequestered beings living between steel walls!
They did not have, to sustain them, as their superiors had, any
of the responsibilities which make up the interest of life, or the
stimulus that comes from having to decide serious questions.
They knew nothing, they saw nothing, not even the sinister coast
in the distance. In spite of the heat of a Chinese summer, fires
were burning day and night in their stifling quarters; they lived
bathed in a moist heat, dripping with perspiration, coming out
only for exhausting drill-work in small boats, in bad weather,
and often in the dead of night and on boisterous seas.

One needs but a glance at their thin pale faces now, to
understand how difficult their obscure rôle has been.

But if I had told of the monotony of their hardships, and
of their silent unending devotion, no one would have had the
patience to read me.

PIERRE LOTI.

Translator's Note

The account of his experiences in China, published by Pierre Loti under the title of "Les Derniers Jours de Pékin," first appeared in the form of letters written to the "Figaro" from China, from notes taken on the spot during those memorable days when he was serving on board one of the French warships.

Loti has written little of late, having had no end of trouble with his naval superiors, through jealousy, it is said, of his literary success.

As Julian Viaud, Loti ranks in the navy as "Lieutenant de vaisseau." Some time ago he was abruptly retired. He took his case before the "Conseil d'état," which finally gave a verdict in his favor, and he secured the nomination of officier d'ordonnance at the time of the Chinese difficulties, during which he resumed his literary work neglected in a measure on account of the tribulations connected with his naval career.

His account of his experiences in China is very personal and very national, yet, exotic that it is, it presents such a vivid picture of certain phases of China that it is of value as the contribution of an observer possessing sympathy, imagination, and knowledge, as well as the literary sense, to the history of our own times.

MYRTA L. JONES.

Contents

Illustrations

Chapter I

The Arrival in the Yellow Sea

MONDAY, Sept. 24, 1900.

VERY EARLY MORNING, on a calm sea and under a starry sky. A light on the eastern horizon shows that day is about to break, yet it is still night. The air is soft and moist. Is it the summer of the North, or the winter of a warm climate? Nothing in sight on any side, no land, no light, no sail, no indication of any place — just a marine solitude in ideal weather and in the mystery of the wavering dawn.

Like a leviathan which conceals itself in order to surprise, the big iron-clad advances silently with determined slowness, its engines barely revolving.

It has just covered five thousand miles almost without pausing to breathe, constantly making forty-eight turns of the screw to a minute, accomplishing without stopping and without damage of any sort, and without much wear and tear of its substantial machinery, the longest journey, at the highest rate of sustained speed, that a monster of its size has ever undertaken, thus defeating in this important test ships reputed to be faster, and which at first sight might be thought superior in speed.

This morning it has arrived at the end of its journey, it is about to reach a part of the world whose name but yesterday was unknown, but toward which the eyes of Europe are now turning. This sea, where the morning light is calmly breaking, is the Yellow Sea, it is the gulf of Petchili, from which one reaches Pekin. An immense fighting squadron must already be assembled very near us, although as yet nothing indicates its vicinity.

We have been two or three days crossing this Yellow Sea in beautiful September weather. Yesterday and the day before, junks with sails of matting have crossed our route, on their way to Corea; shores and islands more or less distant have appeared, but at the present moment the entire circle of the horizon is empty.

Since midnight we have been moving slowly, in order that our expected arrival in the midst of this fleet of ships — which is to be attended with obligatory military pomp — should not take place at too early an hour.

Five o'clock. Out of the semi-obscurity sounds the music of the reveille, the gay trumpeting, which each morning arouses the sailors. It is earlier than usual, so that there may be ample time to perform the toilet of the iron-clad, which has lost some of its freshness during forty-five days at sea. We still see nothing but empty space, and yet the lookout, from his post aloft, reports black smoke on the horizon. This small cloud of coal smoke, which from below looks like nothing, betokens a formidable presence; it is produced by great steel ships, it is the breath of this unprecedented squadron which we are about to join.

Before the ship's toilet comes that of the crew. Barefooted and bare-chested, the sailors splash in the water in the dawning light. In spite of continual hard work, they are no more tired than the ship that carries them. The *Redoutable* is, of all the ships that departed so suddenly, the only one which has had neither death nor sickness on board, even in crossing the Red Sea.

Now the sun has risen clear above the horizon, a yellow disk which slowly climbs upward from behind the quiet waters. For us, who have just left equatorial regions, this rising, luminous as it is, has I know not what of melancholy and of dulness, which savors of autumn and a northern climate. Really in two or three days the sun has changed. Now it no longer burns, it is no longer dangerous, we cease to fear it.

In front of us, from out the cloud of coal smoke, far-off objects begin to emerge, perceptible only to the eye of the mariner; a forest of spears, one should say, planted away off at the end of space, almost beyond the range of vision. We know what they are, — the giant chimneys, the heavy fighting masts, the terrible paraphernalia of warfare, which, with the smoke, reveal from afar the modern squadron. When our morning cleaning is over, when everything has been washed with buckets of sea water, the *Redoutable* increases her speed to the average of eleven and a half knots an hour, which she has maintained since her departure from France. And while the sailors are busy making the brass and copper shine, she begins again to trace her deep furrow through the tranquil waters.

Objects on the smoky horizon line begin to stand forth and take shape. Below the innumerable masts, masses of every form and color are distinguishable. These are the ships themselves. Between the calm water and the pale sky lies the whole terrible company, an assemblage of strange monsters, some white and yellow, others white and black, others the color of slime or of fog, in order to make them less easily distinguishable. Their backs are humped and their sides half submerged and hidden like big uneasy turtles. Their structures vary according to the conceptions of different persons in regard to engines of destruction, but all alike breathe forth horrible coal smoke, which dulls the morning light.

No more of the coast of China is visible than if we were a thousand leagues away or than if it did not exist. Yet we are close to Taku, the meeting-place toward which for so many days our minds have been bent. It is China, close by although invisible, which attracts by its nearness this herd of beasts of prey, and which keeps them as immovable as fallow deer at bay, at this precise point on the seas, until some one speaks the word.

The water, here where it is less deep, has lost its beautiful blue, to which we have so long been accustomed, and has become troubled and yellow, and the sky, although cloudless, is decidedly melancholy. Our first impression of this whole scene, of which we shall undoubtedly for a long time form a part, is one of sadness.

But now as we draw nearer and the sun rises there is a change, and the beautiful shining ironclads with their many-colored flags begin to stand out. It is indeed a remarkable squadron that here represents Europe, — Europe armed against gloomy old China. It occupies an infinite amount of space, the whole horizon seems crowded with ships, and small boats — little steam tugs — hurry like busy people among the big motionless vessels.

Now cannon on all sides begin a military welcome for our admiral, beneath the heavy curtain of black smoke; the gay light smoke from powder blossoms like sheaves and goes off in white masses, while up and down the iron masts the tricolor rises and falls in our honor. Everywhere trumpets sound, foreign bands play our Marseillaise, — one is more or less intoxicated with this ceremonial, always the same yet always superb, which here borrows an unaccustomed magnificence on account of the display of the fleet.

And now the sun is at last awake and shining, adding to the day of our arrival a last illusion of midsummer heat, in this country of extreme seasons; in two months' time it will begin to freeze up for a long winter.

When evening comes, our eyes, which will weary of it soon enough, are feasted upon a grand fairy-like spectacle, given for us by the squadron. Suddenly electric lights appear on all sides, white, or green, or red, twinkling and sparkling in a dazzling manner; the big ships, by means of a play of lights, converse with one another, and the water reflects thousands of signals, thousands of lights, while the rockets race for the horizon or pass through the sky like delirious comets. One forgets all that breeds death and destruction in this phantasmagoria, and for the moment feels oneself in the midst of a great city, with towers, minarets, palaces, improvised in this part of the world especially for this extravagant nocturnal celebration.

September 25.

It is only the next day and yet everything is different. A breeze came up in the morning, — hardly a breeze, just enough to spread over the sea big vague plumes of smoke. Already furrows are being made in this open and not very deep roadstead, and the small boats, continually going and coming, bob up and down bathed in spray.

A ship with the German colors appears upon the horizon just as we appeared yesterday; it is immediately recognized as the *Herta*, bringing Field-Marshal von Waldersee, the last one of the military commanders expected at this meeting-place of the Allies. The salutes that yesterday were for us, begin anew for him, the whole magnificent ceremony is repeated. Again the cannon give forth clouds of smoke, mingling tufts of white with the denser variety, and the national air of Germany is taken up by all the bands, and borne on the rising wind.

The wind whistles stronger, stronger and colder; a bad autumn wind, that plays about the whalers and the tugs, which yesterday circulated readily among the various groups of the squadron.

It presages difficult days for us, for in this uncertain harbor, which in an hour's time becomes dangerous, we shall have to land thousands of soldiers sent from France and thousands of tons of war supplies. Many people and many things must be moved over this rough water, in barges or in small boats, in the cold and even in the night, and must be taken to Taku across the river's changing bar.

To organize this long and perilous undertaking is to be our task — that of the marines — during the first few months, an austere, exhausting, and obscure rôle without apparent glory.

Chapter II

At Ning-Hia

Oct. 3, 1900.

In the gulf of Petchili on the beach at Ning-Hia, lighted by the rising sun. Here are sloops, tugs, whalers, junks, their prows in the sand, landing soldiers and war supplies at the foot of an immense fort whose guns are silent. On this shore there is a confusion and a babel such as has been seen in no other epoch of history. From these boats where so many people are disembarking, float pell-mell all the flags of Europe.

The shore is wooded with birches and willows, and in the distance mountains with strange outlines raise their peaks to the clear sky. There are only northern trees, showing that the winters in this country are cold, and yet the morning sun is already burning; the far-off peaks are magnificently violet, the sun shines as in Provence. Standing about among the sacks of earth collected for the erection of hasty defences, are all kinds of people. There are Cossacks, Austrians, Germans, English midshipmen, alongside of our armed sailors; little Japanese soldiers, with a surprisingly good military bearing in their new European uniforms; fair ladies of the Russian Red-Cross Society, busy unpacking material for the ambulances; and Bersaglieri from Naples, who have put their cockfeathers onto colonial caps.

There is something about these mountains in this sunshine, in this limpid air, that recalls the shores of the Mediterranean

on autumn mornings. Not far away an old gray structure rises among the trees, twisted, crooked, bristling with dragons and monsters. It is a pagoda. The interminable line of ramparts which winds about and finally loses itself behind the summits of the mountains in the distance, is the Great Wall of China, which forms the boundary of Manchuria.

The soldiers who disembark barefooted in the sand, gaily calling out to one another in all tongues, seem to be the sort who are easily amused. What they are doing to-day is called "a peaceful capture," and it seems more like a celebration of universal fusion, of universal peace, yet not far from here, in the vicinity of Tien-Tsin and of Pekin, the country is in ruins and is strewn with the dead.

The necessity for occupying Ning-Hia, of holding it as a base of supplies, had been impressed upon the admirals of the international squadron, and day before yesterday all the ships had prepared for a struggle, knowing that the forts on the shore were well armed; but the Chinese who lived here, warned by an official that a formidable company of cuirassiers would appear at daybreak, preferred to leave the place — so we found it deserted on our arrival.

The fort which overlooks the shore and which forms the terminus of the Great Wall at its sea end, has been declared international.

The flags of the seven allied nations float there together, arranged in alphabetical order at the end of long poles guarded by pickets, — Austria, France, Germany, Great Britain, Italy, Japan, Russia.

The other forts scattered over the surrounding heights have been apportioned, the one belonging to France being situated about a mile from the shore. It is reached by a dusty road, bordered with birches and frail willows, which crosses gardens

and orchards turning brown at the same season as our own, —
gardens exactly like ours, with modest rows of cabbages and
pumpkins and long lines of lettuce. The little wooden houses
too, scattered here and there among the trees, resemble those of
our villages, with red tiled roofs, vines trained in garlands, and
little beds of zinnias, asters, and chrysanthemums. It is a country
which should be peaceful, happy, yet which has in two days'
time become depopulated through fear of the approach of the
invaders from Europe.

On this fresh October morning the sailors and soldiers of
all nations are hurrying and skurrying along the shaded road
that leads to the French fort, seeking the pleasures of discovery;
amusing themselves in a conquered land, catching chickens and
pilfering salads and pears from the gardens. The Russians are
taking down the Buddhas and gilded vases from a pagoda. The
English are driving with sticks the cattle captured in the fields.
The Dalmatians and the Japanese — fast friends of an hour's
standing — are making their toilet together on the banks of a
stream, and two Bersaglieri who have caught a little donkey are
riding it astride, almost bursting with laughter.

And yet the sad exodus of Chinese peasants which began
yesterday still continues; in spite of the assurance given them
that no harm would be done to any one, those who were left
felt themselves too near and preferred to flee. Whole families
departed with bowed heads; men, women, children, all dressed
alike in blue cotton gowns, and loaded with baggage, even the
babies resignedly carrying their little pillows and mattresses.

One scene was heart-breaking. An old Chinese woman —
very, very old, perhaps a hundred years old — who could scarcely
stand up, was going, God knows where, driven from her home,
where a company of Germans had established themselves; she
went away, dragging herself along with the help of two young

lads who may have been her grandsons and who supported her as best they could, looking at her with infinite respect and tenderness. Seeming not to see us and looking as though she had nothing further to expect from any one, she passed slowly by, her poor face filled with despair, with supreme and irremediable distress, whilst the soldiers behind her were throwing away with shouts of laughter the unpretentious images from the altar of her ancestors. The beautiful sunshine of the autumn morning shone calmly on her well-cared-for little garden, blooming with zinnias and asters.

The fort which fell to the lot of the French occupies almost the space of a town with all its dependencies, lodgings for mandarins and soldiers, electrical work-shops, stables, and powder magazines. In spite of the dragons that adorn the gates and in spite of the clawed monster painted on a stone slab in front of the entrance, it is constructed upon the most recent principles — plastered, casemated, and provided with Krupp guns of the latest models. Unfortunately for the Chinese, who had accumulated in the vicinity of Ning-Hia some terrifying defences, — mines, torpedoes, fougades, and intrenched camps, — nothing was finished, nothing completed anywhere; the movement against foreigners began six months too soon, before they had gotten into working order all the material Europe had sold to Li-Hung-Chang.

A thousand Zouaves who are to arrive to-morrow are to occupy this fort during the winter; while awaiting their arrival we have simply brought along a score of sailors to take possession.

It is curious to go among these houses, abandoned in haste and terror, and to find ourselves in the midst of the disorder of precipitate flight; broken furniture and dishes, clothing, guns, bayonets, ballistic books, boots with paper soles, umbrellas, and ambulance supplies are piled pell-mell before the doors. In the kitchens dishes of rice are ready for the oven, with plates of cabbage and cakes made of fried grasshoppers.

There are shells everywhere, cartridges strew the grounds, gun-cotton is dangerously dispersed, and black powder is scattered in long trains. But side by side with this debauch of war materials, droll details attest the human side of Chinese life; on all the window-sills are pots of flowers, on all the walls are household gods placed there by the soldiers. The familiar sparrow abounds here, and is never interfered with, it seems, by the inhabitants of the place, and from the roofs the cats, circumspect but anxious to enter into relations with us, are observing the sort of *ménage* that will be possible with such unexpected hosts as ourselves.

Very near us, a hundred metres from our fort, passes the Great Wall of China. It is surmounted at this point by a watch tower, where the Japanese are now established, and there they have planted their white flag on a bamboo stick in the red sunlight.

Always smiling, especially at the French, the little Japanese soldiers invite us to come up to see from above the surrounding country.

The Great Wall, seven or eight hundred metres thick at this point, descends gently amid green grass on the Chinese side, but drops vertically on the side toward Manchuria, where it is flanked by enormous square bastions.

We mount, and at our feet we see the wall plunging on one hand into the Yellow Sea, while on the other it rises to the summits of the mountain and goes winding on through the fields as far as the eye can see, giving the impression of a colossal thing which never comes to any end.

Toward the east we have a view, in this clear light, of the deserted plains of Manchuria.

Toward the west — in China — the wooded country has a deceptive look of peace and confidence. All the European flags hoisted on the forts have a festive air amid all the green. It is true that on a plain near the shore there are evidences of an immense movement of Cossacks, but they are far away and the noise does not reach us, though there are at least five thousand men among the tents and among the flags which are stuck into the ground. Where the other powers send to Ning-Hia only a few companies, the Russians on the contrary proceed in great masses, because of their designs on neighboring Manchuria. Shan-Hai-Kouan, the Tartar village which has closed its gates through fear of pillage, appears in the distance, gray and mute as though asleep behind its high crenellated walls. On the sea off toward the horizon, rests the squadron of the Allies, — a fleet of steel monsters with black smoke, friends for the moment, silently assembled in the motionless blue.

The weather is calm, exquisite, buoyant. The prodigious rampart of China blossoms at this season like a garden. Between its sombre bricks, loosened by time, asters, and quantities of pinks like those at the seashore in France are pushing their way through.

This legendary wall, which has for centuries stopped all invasion from the north, will probably nevermore see the yellow flag and the green dragon of the Celestial emperors. Its time has gone by, passed, is forever at an end.

CHAPTER III

ON THE WAY TO PEKIN

I
THURSDAY, Oct. 11, 1900.

AT NOON, on a beautiful calm day that is almost warm and very luminous on the water, I leave the admiral's ship, the *Redoutable*, to go on a mission to Pekin.

We are in the gulf of Petchili on the road to Taku, but at such a distance from the shore that it is not visible, so there is no indication of China anywhere.

The trip begins with a short ride on a steam launch, which takes us out to the *Bengali*, the little despatch-boat which will bring me to land by to-night.

The water is softly blue in the autumn sunshine, which is always bright in this part of the world. To-day, by chance, the wind and the waves seem to sleep. As far as one can see, great war-ships succeed one another, motionless and menacing. As far as the horizon there are the turrets, the masts, the smoke of the astonishing international squadron with all its train of satellites, torpedo boats, transports, and a legion of packet-boats.

The *Bengali*, upon which I am about to embark for a day, is one of the little French ships carrying troops and war supplies, which for a month past has been painfully and wearisomely going and coming between the transports or freighters arriving from France, and the port of Taku beyond the Pei-Ho bar.

To-day it is full of Zouaves, — brave Zouaves who arrived yesterday from Tunis, careless and happy, bound for this ominous Chinese land. They are crowded on the bridge, packed together, their faces gay and their eyes wide open for a glimpse of China, which has filled their thoughts for weeks and which is now near at hand, just over the horizon.

According to ceremonial custom, the *Bengali,* when it appears, must pass the stern of the *Redoutable* to salute the admiral. The music waits behind the armor, ready to play one of those marches so intoxicating to the sailor. And when we come up close to the big ship, almost under its shadow, all the Zouaves — those destined to return as well as those who must perish — wave their red caps to the sound of the bugle, with hurrahs for the ship, which here represents France to their eyes, and for the admiral, who from the bridge raises his cap in their honor.

At the end of half an hour China appears.

Never has an uglier and more forbidding shore surprised and congealed poor newly arrived soldiers. A low shore, a gray barren land without tree or grass. Everywhere there are forts of colossal size of the same gray as the earth, masses of geometrical outline pierced by embrasures for guns. Never has the approach to a country presented a more extensive or aggressive military array; on both sides of the horrible stream with its muddy waters loom similar forts, giving the impression of a place both terrible and impregnable, giving the impression also that this harbor, in spite of its wretched surroundings, is of the first order of importance, is the key to a great country, and gives access to a city large, rich, and powerful — as Pekin must have been. From a nearer view the walls of the first two forts, stained, full of holes, and ravaged by cannon-balls, bear witness to furious and recent battles.

We know how, on the day Taku was taken, they exhausted their strength on one another. By a miracle, a French shell from the *Lion*

fell right into one of them, causing the explosion of its enormous powder magazine so that the yellow gunners lost their heads. The Japanese then seized this fort and opened an unexpected fire on the one opposite, and immediately the overthrow of the Chinese began. Had it not been for this chance, for this shell, and for this panic, all the European gunners anchored in the Pei-Ho would inevitably have been lost; the landing of the Allies would have been impossible or problematical, and the whole face of the war changed.

We now move up the river through the muddy infected water where impurities of all sorts are floating, as well as the bodies of men and animals. On both of the sombre shores we see by the light of the declining sun a procession of ruins, a uniform black and gray desolation of earth, ashes, and calcined slopes, tumbled walls, and ruins.

On this pestilential river a feverish animation reigns, so that it is difficult for us to make our way through the obstructions. Junks by the hundreds, each flying the colors and having at the stern the name of the nation by whom it is employed — France, Italy, United States, etc. — in big letters above the devilry of the Chinese inscription, besides a numberless flotilla of towing vessels, lighters, colliers, and packets.

On the terrible, steep, muddy banks, amongst filth and dead animals, there is an ant-like activity. Soldiers of all the armies of Europe mingle with coolies driven with sticks, unpacking military stores, tents, guns, wagons, mules, horses. Such a confusion as never was of uniforms, rubbish, cannons, débris, and provisions of all kinds. An icy wind which rises toward evening makes us shiver after the hot sun of the day and brings with it the gloom of winter.

Before the ruins of a quarter where the flag of France is floating, the *Bengali* approaches the lugubrious shore, and our

Zouaves disembark rather discountenanced by the sombre reception given them by China. While waiting for some sort of a shelter to be provided, they light fires on the shore which the wind fans into flame, and there they heat their evening meal in darkness and silence and in the midst of clouds of infected dust.

On the deserted plain from which the dust, the cold, and the squalls come, the black devastated town, overrun with soldiers, extends, breathing pestilence and death.

A small street through its centre, hastily rebuilt in a few days' time with mud, broken timbers, and iron, is lined with dubious-looking taverns. Men from I don't know where, mongrels of every race, sell absinthe, salt-fish, and deadly liquors to the soldiers. There is some drunkenness, and occasionally knives are drawn.

Outside of this improvised quarter Taku no longer exists. Nothing but ruined walls, burned roofs, piles of ashes, and nameless receptacles of filth, wherein are huddled together old clothing, dogs, and human heads covered with hair.

I slept on board the *Bengali*, this hospitality having been extended to me by the commander. Occasional shots break the nocturnal silence, and toward morning I hear — although half asleep — horrible cries uttered by the Chinese on shore.

FRIDAY, October 12.

I rose at daybreak to go and take the train, which still runs as far as Tien-Tsin and even a little beyond. Farther on, the road having been destroyed by Boxers, I shall continue I do not yet know how, either in a Chinese cart, in a junk, or on horseback, and from all accounts cannot count on seeing the great walls of Pekin for six or seven days. I have an order which will secure me rations from the posts along the road, otherwise I should run the risk of dying from hunger in this ravaged land. I have as little baggage as possible, nothing but a light canteen, and but one travelling companion, a faithful servant brought from France.

At the station, where I arrive at sunrise, I find again all yesterday's Zouaves, their knapsacks on their backs. No tickets are necessary for this railway, everything military is carried by right of conquest. Along with Cossack and Japanese soldiers a thousand Zouaves pile into carriages with broken panes through which the wind whistles. I find a place with their officers, and very soon we are calling up memories of Africa, where they have been, and longing for Tunis and Algeria the White.

We are two hours and a half on the road across the mournful plain. At first it was only gray earth as at Taku; then there were reeds and herbage touched with frost. On all sides are immense splashes of red, like blood stains, due to the autumn flowering of a kind of marsh plant. On the horizon of this desert myriads of migratory birds may be seen, rising like clouds, eddying and then falling. The north wind blows and it is very cold.

Soon the plain is peopled with tombs, — tombs without number, all of the same shape, — each one a kind of cone of earth piled up and surmounted by a ball of faience, — some small, like little huts, others as large as camping tents. They are grouped according to families and they are legion. The entire country is a burial-place with a gory look resulting from the splashes of red to which I have referred.

At the stopping-places where the ruined stations are occupied by Cossacks, there are calcined cars — damaged by fire — and locomotives riddled with balls. At other places we do not stop because there is nothing left; the few villages which mark this vicinity are all destroyed.

Tien-Tsin! It is ten o'clock in the morning. Pierced by the cold, we step down amid the clouds of dust which the north wind perpetually scatters over this dried-up country. We are taken in hand by Chinese scouts, who, without even knowing where we want to go, trot off, at full speed, with us in their little carriages. The European streets along which they are running (here called "concessions"), seen through a cloud of blinding dust, have the look of a big city, but the almost luxurious houses are riddled with shells, literally ripped open and without roofs or windows. The shores of the rivers, here as at Taku, are like a fevered babel; thousands of junks lie there, unloading troops, horses, guns. In the streets where Chinese workmen are carrying enormous loads of war supplies, one meets soldiers of all the nations of Europe, officers in every sort of uniform, on horseback, in chairs, or on foot. And there is of course a perpetual interchange of military salutes.

Where are we to lay our heads? Really, we have no idea, in spite of our desire for a shelter from the icy wind and dust. However, our Chinese runners keep on like rolling balls.

We knock at the doors of two or three hotels which have risen up among the ruins out of a confusion of broken furniture. Everything is full, full to overflowing; gold will not buy a loft with a mattress.

Willy-nilly we must beg our board and lodging from unknown officers, who give us the most friendly hospitality in houses where the holes made by shot and shell have been hastily stopped up so that the wind may no longer enter.

SATURDAY, October 13.

I have chosen to travel by junk as far as the course of the Pei-Ho will permit, the junk serving as a lodging in this country where I am forced to dally.

This makes necessary many little preparations.

The first thing is to make a requisition for this junk and to appropriate this species of sarcophagus where I am to live under a roof of matting. The next is to buy in the more or less ruined shops of Tien-Tsin the things necessary for a few days of nomadic life, from bedding to arms; and lastly, to hire from the Lazarist Fathers a Chinese person to make tea, — young Toum, aged fourteen, with the face of a cat and a queue reaching to the ground.

I dined with General Frey, who, with his small French detachment, was, as every one knows, the first to enter the heart of Pekin, the Imperial City. He was good enough to relate to me in detail this magnificent journey, the taking of the Marble Bridge and his final entrance into the Imperial City, — that mysterious place which I shall soon see, and into which before him no European had ever penetrated.

As to my own small personal expedition, which in comparison with his appears so easy and unimportant, the general kindly concerned himself with what we were to drink *en route*, my servant and I, in this time of infection, when the water is a constant danger on account of human remains, thrown there by the Chinese, left lying in all the wells; and he made me a present of untold value, — a case of eau d'Evian.

II

THE TWO GODDESSES OF THE BOXERS
SUNDAY, October 14.

AN OLD CHINESE woman, wrinkled as a winter apple, timidly opens the door at which we have loudly knocked. It stands in the deep shadow of a narrow passageway exhaling unhealthy fetid smells, between walls blackened by filth, where one feels as shut in as in the heart of a prison.

The old woman, an enigmatical figure, looks us all over with a blank impenetrable gaze; then recognizing among us the chief of the international police, she silently steps aside and permits us to enter. We follow her into a dark little court. Poor late autumn flowers are growing in the old walls, and we breathe faint sickly odors.

We are a group of officers, three French, two English, and one Russian, who are there clearly by right of conquest.

Our conductor is a strange creature, balancing on the tips of her incredibly small feet. Her gray hair fastened with long pins is so tightly drawn back that it seems to raise her eyes unduly. Her dark dress is indefinite in color, but her parchment-like face bears to a high degree that something appertaining to a worn-out race, which we are wont to call distinction. She appears to be only a servant, yet her aspect, her carriage, are disconcerting; some mystery broods over her, she seems like a refined matron who has resorted to a shameful clandestine occupation. This whole place, moreover, is difficult to describe to those who do not know it.

Beyond the court is a sordid vestibule, then a door painted black, with a Chinese inscription consisting of two big red letters. Without knocking, the old woman draws the bolt and opens it.

We may be mistaken, but we have come in all good faith to pay a visit to *two goddesses*, — prisoners kept shut up in this palace. For here we are in the common, the lower dependencies, the secret places of the palace of the viceroy of Petchili, and to reach this spot we have had to pass over the immense desolation of a town with cyclopean walls which is at present only a mass of débris and dead bodies.

The animation of these ruins, accidentally peopled by joyous soldiers, is singular, unique, on this Sunday, which is a holiday in camp and barracks. In the long streets filled with wreckage of all kinds, Zouaves and African chasseurs, arm-in-arm with Germans in pointed helmets, pass gaily between the walls of roofless houses. There are little Japanese soldiers, shining and automatic, Russians with flat caps, plumed Bersaglieri, Austrians, Americans with big felt hats, and Indian cavalrymen with enormous turbans. All the flags of Europe are floating over the ruins of Tien-Tsin, which has been partitioned by the allied armies. In certain quarters the Chinese who have gradually returned, after their flight, have established bazars in the open air in the lovely sunshine of this autumn Sunday, — bazars where in the midst of incendiary ashes they sell to the soldiers articles picked up in the ruins, porcelains, jars, silk dresses, furs. There are so many of these soldiers, so many uniforms of every kind on our route, so many sentinels presenting arms, that we grow weary returning the many salutes received as we pass through this unheard-of babel.

At the farther side of the destroyed city, near the high ramparts in front of the palace of the viceroy, where we are going to see the goddesses, some Chinese, undergoing torture in a kind of pillory, are lined up along the wall, with inscriptions above them describing their offences. Two pickets guard the doors with bayonetted guns, one an American, the other a Japanese, standing alongside of the horrible grinning old stone monsters who watch, crouching, on either side of the entrance.

There is nothing sumptuous, nothing great in this dusty, decrepit palace which we have traversed unheeding, but it speaks of real China, of old China, grimacing and hostile. There is a profusion of monsters in marble, in broken faience, and in worm-eaten wood, falling to pieces from sheer old age or threatening from the edges of roofs to do so; frightful forms half buried in sand and ashes, with horns, claws, forked tongues, and big squinting eyes.

In the grim walled court a few late roses are still in blossom under trees a century old.

Now, after various turns along badly lighted passages, we

reach the goddesses' door, — the one marked with two big red letters. The old Chinese woman, ever mute and mysterious, with head held high but with lifeless eyes persistently downcast, pushes open the black doors, with a gesture of submission which means: "Here they are, look at them!"

In a room which is almost dark and where the evening sun never enters, two poor girls, two sisters who look alike, are seated with bowed heads amid lamentable disorder, in positions indicative of supreme consternation, — one on a chair, the other on the edge of an ebony bed which they must share at night. They are dressed in humble black, but here and there on the floor are scattered shining silks and tunics embroidered in big flowers and gold chimeras, — the garments they put on when going to meet the armies, in the midst of whistling bullets on days of battle, — their attire as warriors and goddesses.

For they are a kind of Jeanne d'Arc, — if it is not blasphemy to pronounce a name of almost ideal purity in this connection, — they are the goddesses of the incomprehensible Boxers, so atrocious and at the same time so admirable: hysterical creatures, exciting both the hatred and terror of the foreigner, who one day fled without fighting in a panic of fear, and the next with the shrieks of the possessed threw themselves straight into the face of death, under a shower of bullets from troops ten times as numerous as themselves.

The goddesses, taken prisoners, are the property, the curious bibelot, if one may use the word, of the seven Allies. They are not badly treated. They are merely shut up for fear they will commit suicide, which has become a fixed idea with them. What will be their fate? Already their captors are tired of seeing them and don't know what to do with them.

On a day of defeat the junk in which they sought refuge was surrounded, and they, with their mother, who followed them everywhere, threw themselves into the water. The soldiers fished them out fainting. The goddesses after much care came to their senses. But the mamma never again opened her oblique old Chinese eyes. The girls were made to believe that she had been taken to a hospital and would soon come back. At first the prisoners were brave, animated, haughty, and always well dressed. But this very morning they have been told that their mother is no more, and it is that which has stunned them, like a physical blow.

Having no money to buy mourning dress, which in China is always white, they asked to be allowed white leather shoes — which at this moment cover their doll-like feet, and which are as essential here as the crape veil is with us.

They are both slender and of a waxen pallor, scarcely pretty, but with a certain grace, a certain charm as they stand there, one in front of the other, without tears, with drooping eyes and with arms falling straight at their sides. They do not raise their eyes even to ascertain who enters or what is wanted of them. They do not stir as we come in, nothing matters to them now. They await death, indifferent to everything.

They inspire in us an unlooked-for respect by the dignity of their despair, respect and infinite compassion. We have nothing to say to one another, and are as embarrassed at being there as though we had been guilty of some indiscretion.

It occurred to us to put some money on the disordered bed; but one of the sisters, while appearing not to see us, threw the pieces of silver onto the floor and with a gesture invited the servant to dispose of them as she wished. So that this was on our part a further mistake.

There is such an abyss of misunderstanding between European officers and Boxer goddesses that it is impossible to show our sympathy for them in any way. So we, who came to be amused by a curious sight, depart in silence with a tightening of the heartstrings at the thought of the two poor creatures imprisoned in a gloomy room in the fading evening light.

My junk, with five Chinese aboard, will go up the river under the French flag, which is already a protection. The war department has decided it to be more prudent — although my servant and I are armed — to send two soldiers with us, two men with horses carrying guns and munitions.

Beyond Tien-Tsin, where I have spent another day, one may go an hour further by train in the direction of Pekin, as far as the town of Yang-Soon. My junk, with two soldiers, Toum, and the baggage, will await me there at a bend in the river, and has gone on ahead to-day with a military escort.

I dine this evening with the consul-general, the one who escaped being shot almost by miracle, although his flag was for a long time, during the siege, a mark for the Chinese gunners.

III

MONDAY, October 15.

I Left Tien-Tsin by railway at eight o'clock in the morning. An hour on the road, across the same old plain, the same desolation, the same cutting wind, the same dust. Then the ruins of Yang-Soon, where the train stops because there is no road left; from this point on, the Boxers have destroyed everything, the bridges are cut, the stations burned, and the rails scattered over the country.

My junk is there awaiting me by the river's side. For the present, for three days at least, I must arrange for a life on the water, in the little sarcophagus which is the cabin of this queer boat, under the roof of matting which gives a view of the sky through a thousand holes, and which tonight will permit the white frost to disturb our slumbers. But this room in which I am to live, eat and sleep in complete promiscuity with my French companions is so small, so very small that I dismiss one of the soldiers. We could never manage there with four.

The Chinese of my train, ragged and sordid, receive me with profound bows. One takes the rudder, the others jump onto the bank, where they harness themselves to the end of a long line attached to the mast of the junk — and we are off, being towed against the current of the Pei-Ho, a heavy poisonous stream in which, here and there amongst the reeds on the banks, parts of human bodies appear.

The soldier I have kept is named Renaud, and he tells me he comes from Calvados. He and my servant Osman, both happy to be going to Pekin, vie with one another in gaiety and good-will and in comical ingenious inventions to make our lodging more convenient. The trip, in spite of unpleasant surroundings, begins to the sound of their merry childlike laughter. We depart in the full morning-light, under the rays of a deceptive sunshine which pretends it is summer although an icy wind is blowing.

The seven allied nations have established military posts from point to point along the Pei-Ho, to insure communication by way of the river between Pekin and the gulf of Petchili, where their ships come in. Toward eleven o'clock I stop the junk near a large Chinese fort from which floats the French flag.

It is one of our posts occupied by Zouaves; we get out to get our rations, enough bread, wine, preserves, sugar, and tea for two days. We shall receive no more now until Tong-Tchow (City of Celestial Purity), which we shall reach day after to-morrow in the evening, if nothing untoward prevents. Then the towing of our junk begins again; slowly and monotonously we move between gloomy devastated banks.

The country around us remains unchanged. On both sides as far as the eye can reach are fields of "sorghos" — which is a kind of giant millet much taller than our maize. The war prevented its being harvested in season, and so it stands reddened by the frost. The monotonous little tow-path, a narrow strip on the grayish soil, is on a level with the cold fetid water, at the foot of the eternal dried sorghos, which forms an endless curtain all along the river. Sometimes a phantom village appears on the horizon; as one approaches it, it proves to be only ruins and the bodies of the dead.

I have a mandarin's arm-chair in my junk on which to enthrone myself when the sun shines and the wind is not too cutting. More frequently I prefer to walk along the shore doing my miles in company with our towers, who plod along bending over like beasts of burden, with the rope passed over the shoulders. Osman and Renaud peer out of a port-hole after me as we walk along the track of gray earth shut in by the uninterrupted border of sorghos and by the river, the wind blowing sharply all the while. We are often obliged to step aside suddenly because of a dead man — with one leg stretched out across the path — looking slyly up at us.

The events of the day are the meeting of junks going down the river and passing ours. They go in long lines fastened together, flying the flag of some one of the allied nations, and carrying the sick, the wounded, and the spoils of war.

In the twilight we pass the remains of a village in which the Russians, on their way to Manchuria, are encamped for the night. They are taking carved furniture out of an abandoned house, breaking it up and making a fire of it. As we go on we see the flames mounting in great jets, and reaching out to the sorghos near by; for a long time its incendiary light is visible behind us, in the mournful empty grayness of the distance. This first nightfall on our junk is full of gloom in the strange solitude into which hour by hour we penetrate still further. The shadows are deep about us and there are many dead along the ground. In the confused and infinite darkness, all about us seems hostile or gloomy, and the cold increases with the silence and obscurity.

The impression of melancholy disappears at supper when our Chinese lantern is lighted, illuminating the sarcophagus, which we have closed as tightly as possible to shut out the wind. I have invited my two companions to my table — my comical little table, which they themselves have made from a broken oar and an old plank. The bread seems exquisite to us after our long walk on the bank; to warm us we have the hot tea which young Toum has prepared for us over a fire of sorghos, and when hunger is assuaged and Turkish cigarettes give forth their soothing clouds of smoke, we have almost a feeling of home and comfort in our poor shelter enveloped in outside darkness.

Then comes bedtime — although the junk moves on, our towers continuing their march by feeling their way along the sorghos of the dark path, so full of surprises. Toum, although he is an elegant young Chinaman, goes to roost with the others of his race in the straw in the hold. The rest of us, still dressed of course, with our boots on and firearms at hand, stretch out on the narrow camp-bed of our cabin, looking at the stars, which, as soon as the lantern is out, appear between the meshes of our matting-roof, shining brightly in the frosty sky.

Distant shots reach us from far off, indicating nocturnal dramas with which we have no concern, and just before midnight two guards, one Japanese and the other German, try to stop our junk; we are obliged to get up to discuss the matter, and by means of a hastily lighted lantern, show the French flag and the stripes that I wear on my sleeve.

At midnight the Chinese make fast our boat, at a spot they say is safe, so that they too may rest. We all fall into a profound slumber in the icy night.

IV

TUESDAY, October 16.

WE ARE UP at daylight and off again. In the cold, magnificent dawn, upon a clear pink sky, the sun rises and shines without heat on the green plain, and on the deserted place where we have slept.

All at once I leap to the ground with an instinctive longing for activity, anxious to move, to walk. Horrors! At a turn in the path as I am running fast without looking where I am going, I almost step on something in the form of a cross, — a naked corpse lying face downward with extended arms, half buried in the mud and of a corresponding color; the dogs or the crows, or some Chinese who wanted the queue, have taken the scalp, leaving the cranium white and minus hair or skin.

It grows colder each day as we get farther away from the sea, and the plain begins gradually to slope upward.

Junks pass as they did yesterday, going down the river in files with military stores, and are under the care of soldiers of all the nations of Europe. Then come long intervals of solitude, during which no living thing appears in this region of millet and reeds. The wind that blows more and more bitterly is healthful; it dilates the chest, and for the moment redoubles life. So we march along between the sorghos and the river, on the everlasting frosty path that leads to Pekin, without fatigue, without any desire to hurry, but always ahead of the solemn Chinamen, who, tugging at their ropes, continue to draw our floating house, keeping up their pace with the regularity of machines.

There are a few trees now on the banks, willows with very green leaves of a variety unknown to us; they seem untouched by the autumn, and their beautiful color is in striking contrast to the rusty tones of the grass and the dying sorghos. There are gardens too, — abandoned gardens that belonged to hamlets that have been burned; our Chinamen sometimes send one of their number on a marauding expedition, and he brings back armfuls of vegetables for our meals.

Osman and Renaud, as we pass by ruined houses, sometimes pick up articles which they think necessary for the embellishment of our dwelling, — small mirrors, carved seats, lanterns, even bunches of artificial flowers made of rice paper, which may have adorned the headdresses of massacred or fleeing Chinese ladies, and which they naively use to decorate the walls of the room. The interior of our sarcophagus soon takes on an air of distinction quite droll and barbaric.

It is astonishing how soon we accustom ourselves to the perfectly simple life on the junk, an existence of healthy fatigue, devouring appetites, and heavy sleep.

Toward the evening of this day the mountains of Mongolia, those which tower above Pekin, begin to appear on the distant horizon, on the very border of this infinitely level land.

There is something especially lugubrious about the twilight to-day. The sinuous Pei-Ho, narrowing hour by hour at each turn, seems to be but a tiny stream between its silent shores, and we feel altogether too much shut in by the confused growth which conceals such sombre things. The day goes out in one of those cold dead colorings that are a specialty of Northern winters. All that there is in the way of light comes from the water, which reflects more vividly than the sky; the river, like a mirror, reflects the sunset yellows; one might even say that it exaggerates the sad light, as it runs between the inverted images of the reeds, the monotonous sorghos and the already black silhouettes of the few trees. The solitude is deeper than that of yesterday. The cold and the silence settle down upon one like a winding sheet. There is a penetrating melancholy in feeling the slow oncoming of the night in this nameless spot, a certain anguish in looking at the last reflections of the neighboring reeds, — reflections which continue, even though ahead of us darkness claims the hostile and unknown distance.

Happily, the hour for supper is here, the longed-for hour, for we are very hungry. In our little retreat I shall find again the red light of our lantern, the excellent soldier's bread, the smoking tea served by Toum, and the cheerfulness of my two good servants.

Toward nine o'clock, just as we pass a group of junks full of people, all Chinese, — marauders' junks evidently, — we hear cries behind us, — cries of distress and death, cries that are horrible in the stillness. Toum, who lends his fine ear and understands all that these people are saying, explains that they are engaged in killing an old man because he has stolen some rice. We were not numerous enough or sure enough of our party, to interfere. I fired two shots into the air in their direction, and all became still as if by magic; we had, no doubt, saved the head of the old rice thief at least until the morning.

Then it is quiet until daylight. After midnight, tied up no matter where among the reeds, we all sleep a sleep that is undisturbed. It is calm and cold under the stars. There are a few shots fired in the distance. We are conscious of them, but they do not wake us.

WEDNESDAY, October 17.

We rise at daybreak and run along the bank in the white frost; the dawn is pink, and soon the sun rises bright and clear.

Wishing to take a short cut through the everlasting sorghos fields and to rejoin the junk which is obliged to follow a long turn in the river further on, we cross the ruins of a hamlet where frightfully contorted bodies are lying, on whose blackened members the ice has formed little crystals that shine like a coating of salt.

After our noon dinner, as we emerge from the semi-obscurity of our sarcophagus, the Chinamen point to the horizon. Tong-Tchow, the "City of Celestial Purity," is beginning to show itself; great black walls surmounted with miradors, and an astonishingly tall, slender tower, of a very Chinese outline with twenty superimposed roofs.

It is all distant still, and the plains about us are full of horrors. From a stranded junk emerges a long dead arm, of a bluish tone. And the bodies of cattle borne by the current pass by us in a perfect procession, all swollen and exhaling a bovine pest. A cemetery must have been violated hereabouts, for on the mud of the shore there are empty coffins with human bones alongside them.

V

AT TONG-TCHOW

Tong-tchow, which occupies two or three kilometres along the bank, is one of those immense Chinese cities — more densely populated than many of the capitals of Europe — whose very name is almost unheard of with us. To-day, needless to say, it is but the ghost of a city, and as one approaches it it does not take long to perceive that it is now empty and in ruin.

We approach slowly. At the foot of the high black crenellated walls, junks are crowded all along the river. On the bank the same excitement as at Taku and at Tien-Tsin is complicated by some hundreds of Mongolian camels crouching in the dust.

There are soldiers, invaders, cannons, materials of war. Cossacks who are trying captured horses go and come at full gallop among the various groups, with great savage cries.

The various national colors of the European Allies are hoisted in profusion; they float from high up on the black walls pierced by cannon balls, from the camps, from the junks, from the ruins.

And the continual wind — the implacable icy wind carrying the infected dust that smells of the dead — plays upon these flags, which give an ironical air of festivity to all the devastation.

I look for the French flags so as to stop my junk in our neighborhood and to go at once to our quarters. I can try our country's rations there this evening; furthermore, not being able to continue our trip on the river, I must procure for to-morrow morning a cart and some saddle horses.

Stopping near a place which seems to belong to us, I ask some Zouaves the road to our quarters; they promptly, eagerly, and politely offer to accompany me. Together we go on toward a great door in the thick black wall.

At this entrance to the city they have, by means of ropes and boards, established a cattle-yard for the purpose of supplying food for the soldiers. Besides a few live animals there are three or four on the ground, dead from the bovine pest, and some Chinese prisoners have this moment come to drag them to the river, the general rendezvous for dead bodies.

We enter a street where our soldiers are employed at various kinds of work in the midst of heaps of rubbish. Through the broken doors and windows of the houses the wretched interiors are visible; everything is in fragments, broken, destroyed as though for pleasure. From the thick dust raised by the north wind and by our own footsteps rises an intolerable odor of the dead.

For two months the rage for destruction, the frenzy for murder, has beset this unfortunate "City of Celestial Purity," invaded by the troops of eight or ten different countries. She felt the first shock of all these hereditary hatreds. First the Boxers came her way. Then the Japanese, — heroic little soldiers of whom I do not wish to speak ill, but who destroy and kill as barbarian armies were wont to do. Still less do I wish to speak ill of our friends, the Russians; but they have sent here their Cossack neighbors from Tartary, and half-Mongolian Siberians, all admirable under fire, but looking at war in the Asiatic fashion. Then there are the cruel cavalrymen of India sent by Great Britain. America has let loose her soldiers. And when, in the first desire for vengeance for Chinese cruelties, the Italians, the Germans, the Austrians, and the French arrived, nothing was left intact.

Our commander and his officers have improvised lodgings and offices in some of the larger Chinese houses, hastily repairing the roofs and walls. In strong contrast to the rudeness of these places are the sumptuous wood carvings and the tall Chinese vases found intact among the ruins.

They promise me carriages and horses for to-morrow morning to be ready at sunrise on the bank near my junk. When all is settled there is about an hour of daylight left, so I wander about the ruins of the city with my armed followers, Osman, Renaud, and Chinese Toum.

As one gets farther away from the quarters where our soldiers are, the horrors increase with the solitude and the silence.

We come first to the street of the China merchants, great warehouses where the products of the Canton manufactories were stored. It must have been a fine street judging from the carved and gilded but ruined façades which remain. To-day the yawning shops, almost demolished, seem to vomit onto the highway their heaps of broken fragments. One walks on precious enamel decorated with brilliant flowers, for it literally covers the ground so that one crushes it in passing. There is no knowing whose work this was; it was already done when our troops arrived. But it must have taken whole days of furious attack with boots and clubs to reduce it all to such small bits; jars, plates, cups, are ground to atoms, pulverized, together with human bones and hair. At the back of these warehouses the coarser wares occupied a sort of interior court. These courts with their old walls are particularly lugubrious this evening, in the dying light. In one of them we found a mangy dog trying to drag something from underneath a pile of broken plates — it was the body of a child whose skull had been broken. The dog began to eat the flesh that was left on the legs of the poor dead thing.

There was no one to be seen in the long devastated streets where the framework of the houses, as well as the tiles and the bricks, had tumbled down. Crows croaked in the silence. Horrible dogs who feed on the dead fled before us, hanging their tails. We had glimpses of Chinese prowlers, wretched-looking creatures, trying to find something to steal, or of some of the dispossessed timidly creeping along the walls attempting to find out what has become of their homes.

The sun is already low, and the wind is rising as it does every night. We shiver with the sudden cold. Empty houses fill the shadows.

These houses are all of considerable extent, with recesses, a succession of courts, rock work, basins, and melancholy gardens. Crossing the threshold, guarded by the ever-present granite monsters worn by the rubbing of hands, one finds oneself in an endless series of apartments. The intimate details of Chinese life are touchingly and graciously revealed by the arrangement of potted plants, flowerbeds, and little balconies where bindweed and other vines are trained.

Here, surrounded with playthings, is a poor doll, which doubtless belonged to some child whose head has been broken; there a cage hangs with the bird still in it, dried up in one corner with its feet in the air.

Everything is sacked, removed, or destroyed; furniture is broken, the contents of drawers thrown about the floors, papers, blood-stained clothing, Chinese women's shoes spattered with blood, and here and there limbs, hands, heads, and clumps of hair.

In certain of the gardens neglected plants continue to blossom gaily, running over into the walks amongst the human remains. Around an arbor which conceals the body of a woman, twines pink convolvulus in blossoming garlands. The blossom is still open at this late hour of the day and in spite of the cold nights, which quite upsets our European ideas of convolvulus.

In one of the houses back in a recess in a dark loft, something moves! Two women cower pitifully! Finding themselves discovered, they are seized with terror and fall at our feet, trembling, weeping, clasping their hands, and begging for mercy. One is young, the other older, and they look alike. Mother and daughter! "Pardon, sir, pardon; we are afraid," translates little Toum naively, understanding their broken words. Evidently they expect the worst of us — and then death. For how long have they lived in this hole, these two poor things, thinking with each step that resounds on the pavement of the deserted court that their end has come? We leave them a few pieces of silver, which perhaps humiliates without helping them, but it is all that we can do, and then we go.

Another house, a house of the rich this one is, with a profusion of potted plants in enamelled porcelain jars in the sad little garden. In an apartment that is already dark (for decidedly night is coming on, the uncertainty of twilight is beginning), but where the havoc is less extensive, for there are great chests and beautiful armchairs still intact, Osman suddenly recoils with terror before something which emerges from a bucket placed upon a board. Two torn thighs, the whole lower part of a woman thrust into this bucket with the feet in the air! Undoubtedly the mistress of this elegant home. Her body? Who knows what has been done with the body? But here is the head, under this arm-chair, near the skeleton of a cat. The mouth is open, showing the teeth, and the hair is long.

In addition to the broad, almost straight streets whose desolation is visible from one end to the other, there are little tortuous streets leading up to gray walls. They are the most desolate to enter at this twilight hour, with only the cry of the crow as an accompaniment. Little stone gnomes guard their mysterious doors, and their pavements are strewn with human heads with long queues. One approaches certain turns in the streets with a heavy heart. It is over, and nothing in the world would tempt us to enter again at this hour one of those frightfully still houses where one meets with so many gruesome encounters.

We had gone far into the city before night came on, and the silence had become intolerable. We return to the region where the troops are quartered, cut by the north wind and chilled by the cold and gloom; our return is rapid; broken china and other débris impossible to define crackle under our feet.

The banks are lined with soldiers warming themselves and cooking their suppers over bright fires, where they are burning chairs, tables, and bits of carved wood or timbers. Coming out of the Dantesque streets, it all bespeaks joy and comfort to us.

Near our junk there is a canteen, improvised by a Maltese, where intoxicants are sold to soldiers. I send my men to get whatever liquors they want for our supper, for we need something to warm and cheer us if possible. We celebrate with smoking soup, tea, chartreuse, and I don't know what besides, in our little matting-covered dwelling, tied up this time on the pestilential mud and enveloped as usual by cold and darkness.

At dessert, when the hour for smoking arrives in our sarcophagus, Renaud, to whom I have given the floor, tells us that his squadron is encamped on the borders of a Chinese cemetery in Tien-Tsin, and that the soldiers of another European nation

(I prefer not to say which) in the same vicinity spend their time ransacking the graves and taking from them the money which it is the custom to bury with the dead.

"To me, colonel" (I am colonel to him, as he is ignorant of the naval appellation of *commandant*, which, with us, goes with five gold stripes), "to me it does not seem right. Even though they are Chinese, we ought to leave their dead in peace. What disgusts me is that they cut their rations up on the planks of the coffins. And I say to them, 'Put it on the outside if you will, but not on the inside, which has touched the corpse.' But these savages, colonel, laugh at me."

VI
THURSDAY, October 18.

It is a surprise to awaken to a dark and sombre sky. We counted upon having, as on the preceding mornings, the almost never clouded autumn and winter sun, which in China shines and warms even when everything is frozen hard, and which has, up to this time, helped us to support the gruesome sights of our journey.

When we open the door of the junk just before dawn, our horses and cart are there, having just arrived. On the forbidding shore some Mongolians with their camels are crouched about a fire which has burned all night in the dust; and behind their motionless groups the high walls of the city, of an inky blackness, rise to meet the low-hanging clouds.

We leave our small nomadic equipment in the junk, in the care of two marines of the Tong-Tchow division, who will look after it until our return, and also our most precious possession, the last of the bottles of pure water given us by the general.

The last stage of our journey is made in the company of the French consul-general at Tien-Tsin and of the chancellor of the legation, who are both bound for Pekin, under the escort of a marshal and three or four artillerymen.

Our long, monotonous route leads us across fields of sorghos reddened by the early frosts, and through deserted villages where no one is stirring. It is a cold, gray morning, and the autumn country, upon which a fine rain is falling, is in mourning.

At certain moments I almost fancy myself on the roads of the Basque country in November, amid the uncut maize. Then all at once some unknown symbol arises to recall China, — either a tomb of mysterious shape or a stele mounted upon enormous granite tortoises.

From time to time we meet military convoys of one nation or another, or lines of ambulances. In one place some Russians have taken shelter from a shower in the ruins of a village; in another a number of Americans, who have discovered some hidden clothing in an abandoned house, go on their way rejoicing, with fur mantles on their backs.

Then there are tombs, always tombs, from one end to the other; China is strewn with them; some are almost hidden by the roadside, others are magnificently isolated in enclosures which are like mortuary thickets of dark green cedars.

Ten o'clock. We should be approaching Pekin, although as yet nothing indicates its nearness. We have not seen a single Chinese since our departure; the whole country is deserted and silent under a veil of almost imperceptible rain.

We are going to pass not far from the tomb of an empress, it seems, and the French chancellor, who knows the neighborhood, proposes that he and I make a detour to look at it. So, leaving the others to continue their route, we take a side path through the tall, damp grass.

A canal and a pool soon appear, of a pale color, under the indefinite sky. There is no one to be seen anywhere; the sad quiet of a depopulated country prevails. The tomb on the opposite bank scarcely peeps out from its cedar wood, which is walled about on all sides. We see little but the first marble gates leading to it and the avenue of white stele which is finally lost under the mysterious trees. It is all rather distant, and is reproduced in the mirror of the pool in long inverted reflections. Near us the tall leaden stems of some lotus killed by the frost bend over the water, where the rain drops have traced faint rings. The whitish spheres seen here and there are heads of the dead.

When we rejoin our company they promise that we shall enter Pekin in half an hour. After the complications and delays of our journey we almost believe we shall never arrive. Besides, it is incredible that so large a city could be so near in this deserted country, such a little way ahead of us.

"Pekin does not proclaim itself," explains my new companion. "Pekin takes hold of you; when you perceive it you are there."

The road passes through groups of cedars and willows with falling leaves, and in the concentration of our effort to see the City Celestial we trot on in the fine rain, which does not wet us at all, so drying are the northern winds, carrying the dust always and everywhere; we trot on without speaking.

"Pekin!" suddenly exclaims one of our companions, pointing out an obscure mass just rising above the trees, — a crenellated dungeon of superhuman proportions.

Pekin! In a few seconds, during which I am feeling the spell of this name, a big gloomy wall, of unheard-of height, is disclosed, and goes on endlessly in the gray, empty solitude, which resembles an accursed steppe. It is like a complete change of scene, performed without the noise of machinery or the sounds of an orchestra, in a silence more impressive than any music. We are at the very foot of the bastions and ramparts, dominated by them, although a turn in the road had up to this moment

concealed them. At the same time the rain is turning to snow, whose white flakes mingle with the suspended dirt and dust. The wall of Pekin overwhelms us, a giant thing of Babylonian aspect, intensely black under the dead light of a snowy autumn morning. It rises toward the sky like a cathedral, but it goes on; it is prolonged, always the same, for miles. Not a person on the outskirts of the city, not a green thing all along these walls! The ground is uneven, dusty, ashen in color, and strewn with rags, bones, and even an occasional skull! From the top of each black battlement a crow salutes us as we pass, cawing mournfully.

The clouds are so thick and low that we do not see clearly; we are oppressed by long-looked-for Pekin, which has just made its abrupt and disconcerting appearance above our heads; we advance to the intermittent cries of the crows, rather silent ourselves, overpowered at being there, longing to see some movement, some life, some one or some thing come out from these walls.

From a gate ahead of us, from a hole in the colossal enclosure, slowly emerges an enormous brown, woolly animal like a gigantic sheep; then two, then three, then ten. A Mongolian caravan begins to pass us, always in the same silence, broken only by the croakings of the ravens. These enormous Mongolian camels, with their furry coats, muffs on their legs, and manes like lions, file in an endless procession past our frightened horses. They wear neither bells nor rattles, like the thin beasts of the Arabian deserts; their feet sink deep into the sand, which muffles their footsteps so the silence is not broken by their march.

Perceived through a veil of fine snow and black dust, the caravan has passed us, and moves on without a sound, like a phantom thing. We find ourselves alone again, under this Titanic wall, from which the crows keep watch. And now it is our turn to enter the gloomy city through the gates by which the Mongolians have just passed out.

VII

AT THE FRENCH LEGATION

HERE WE ARE at the gates, the double triple gates, deep as tunnels, and formed of the most powerful masonry, — gates surmounted by deadly dungeons, each one five stories high, with strange curved roofs, — extravagant dungeons, colossal black things above a black enclosing wall.

Our horses' hoofs sink deeper and deeper, disappear, in fact, in the coal-black dust, which is blinding and all-pervading, in the atmosphere as well as on the ground, in spite of the light rain and the snowflakes which make our faces tingle.

Noiselessly, as though we were stepping upon wadding or felt, we pass under the enormous vaults and enter the land of ruin and ashes.

A few slatternly beggars shivering in corners in their blue rags, a few corpse-eating dogs, like those whose acquaintance we have already made en route, — and that is all. Silence and solitude within as well as without these walls. Nothing but rubbish and ruin, ruin.

The land of rubbish and ashes, and little gray bricks, — little bricks all alike, scattered in countless myriads upon the sites of houses that have been destroyed, or upon the pavement of what once were streets.

Little gray bricks, — this is the sole material of which Pekin was built; a city of small, low houses decorated with a lacework of gilded wood; a city of which only a mass of curious débris is left, after fire and shell have crumbled away its flimsy materials.

We have come into the city at one of the corners where there was the fiercest fighting, — the Tartar quarter, which contained the European legations.

Long straight streets may still be traced in this infinite labyrinth of ruins; ahead of us all is gray or black; to the sombre gray of the fallen brick is added the monotonous tone which follows a fire, — the gloom of ashes and the gloom of coal.

Sometimes in crossing the road they form obstacles, — these tiresome little bricks; these are the remains of barricades where fighting must have taken place.

After a few hundred metres we enter the street of the legations, upon which for so many months the anxious attention of the whole world was fixed.

Everything is in ruins, of course; yet European flags float on every piece of wall, and we suddenly find, as we come out of the smaller streets, the same animation as at Tien-Tsin, — a continual coming and going of officers and soldiers, and an astonishing array of uniforms.

A big flag marks the entrance to what was our legation, two monsters in white marble crouch at the threshold; this is the etiquette for all Chinese palaces. Two of our soldiers guard the door which I enter, my thoughts recurring to the heroes who defended it.

We finally dismount, amid piles of rubbish, in an inner square near a chapel, and at the entrance to a garden where the trees are losing their leaves as an effect of the icy winds. The walls about us are so pierced with balls that they look like sieves. The pile of rubbish at our right is the legation proper, destroyed by the explosion of a Chinese mine. At our left is the chancellor's house, where the brave defenders of the place took refuge during the siege, because it was in a less exposed situation. They have offered to take me in there; it was not destroyed, but everything is topsy-turvy, as though it were the day after a battle; and in the room where I am to sleep the plasterers are at work repairing the walls, which will not be finished until this evening.

As a new arrival, I am taken on a pilgrimage to the garden where those of our sailors who fell on the field of honor were hastily buried amid a shower of balls. There is no grass here, no blossoming plants, only a gray soil trampled by the combatants, — crumbling from dryness and cold, — trees without leaves and with branches broken by shot, and over all a gloomy, lowering sky, with snowflakes that are cutting.

We remove our hats as we enter this garden, for we know not upon whose remains we may be treading. The graves will soon be marked, I doubt not, but have not yet been, so one is not sure as one walks of not having under foot some one of the dead who merits a crown.

In this house of the chancellor, spared as by a miracle, the besieged lived helter-skelter, slept on a floor space the size of which was day by day decreased by the damage done by shot and shell, and were in imminent danger of death.

In the beginning — their number, alas, rapidly diminished — there were sixty French sailors and twenty Austrians, meeting death, side by side, with equally magnificent courage. To them were added a few French volunteers, who took their turns on the barricades or on the roofs, and two foreigners, M. and Madame Rosthorn of the Austrian legation. Our officers in command of the defence were Lieutenant Darcy and midshipman Herber; the latter was struck full in the face by a ball, and sleeps to-day in the garden.

The horrible part of this siege was that no pity was to be expected from the besiegers, if, starved, and at the end of their strength, it became necessary for the besieged to surrender, it was death, and death with atrocious Chinese refinements to prolong the paroxysms of suffering.

Neither was there the hope of escape by some supreme sortie; they were in the midst of a swarming city, they were enclosed in a labyrinth of buildings that sheltered a crowd of enemies, and were still further imprisoned by the feeling that, surrounding them, walling in the whole, was the colossal black rampart of Pekin.

It was during the torrid period of the Chinese summer; it was often necessary to fight while dying of thirst, blinded by dust, under a sun as destructive as the balls, and with the constant sickening fear of infection from dead bodies.

Yet a charming young woman was there with them, — an Austrian, to whom should be given one of our most beautiful French crosses. Alone amongst men in distress, she kept an even cheerfulness of the best kind, she cared for the wounded, prepared food for the sick sailors with her own hands, and then went off to aid in carrying bricks and sand for the barricades or to take her turn as watch on the roof.

Day by day the circle closed in upon the besieged as their ranks grew thinner and the garden filled with the dead; gradually they lost ground, although disputing with the enemy, who were legion, every piece of wall, every pile of bricks.

And when one sees their little barricades hastily erected during the night out of nothing at all, and knows that five or six sailors succeeded in defending them (for five or six toward the end were all that could be spared), it really seems as though there were something supernatural about it all. As I walked through the garden with one of its defenders, and he said to me, "At the foot of that little wall we held out for so many days," and "In front of this little barricade we resisted for a week," it seemed a marvellous tale of heroism.

And their last intrenchment! It was alongside the house, — a ditch dug tentatively in a single night, banked up with a few poor sacks of earth and sand; it was all they had to keep out the executioners, who, scarcely six metres away, were threatening them with death from the top of a wall.

Beyond is the "cemetery," that is, the corner of the garden in which they buried their dead, until the still more terrible days when they had to put them here and there, concealing the place for fear the graves would be violated, in accordance with the terrible custom of this place. It was a poor little cemetery whose soil had been pressed and trampled upon in close combat, whose trees were shattered and broken by shell. The interments took place under Chinese fire, and an old whiteheaded priest — since a martyr, whose head was dragged in the gutter — said prayers at the grave, in spite of the balls that whistled about him, cutting and breaking the branches.

Toward the end their cemetery was the "contested region," after they had little by little lost much ground, and they trembled for their dead; the enemy had advanced to its very border; they watched and they killed at close quarters over the sleeping warriors so hastily put to rest. If the Chinese had reached this cemetery, and had scaled the last frail trenches of sand and gravel in sacks made of old curtains, then for all who were left there would have been horrible torture to the sound of music and laughter, horrible dismemberment, — nails torn out, feet torn off, disembowelling, and finally the head carried through the streets at the end of a pole.

They were attacked from all sides and in every possible manner, often at the most unexpected hours of the night. It usually began with cries and the sudden noise of trumpets and tam-tams; around them thousands of howling men would appear, — one must have heard the howlings of the Chinese to imagine what their voices are; their very timbre chills your soul. Gongs outside the walls added to the tumult.

Occasionally, from a suddenly opened hole in a neighboring house, a pole twenty or thirty feet long, ablaze at the end with oakum and petroleum, emerged slowly and silently, like a thing out of a dream. This was applied to the roofs in the hope of setting them on fire.

They were also attacked from below, they heard dull sounds in the earth, and understood that they were being undermined, that their executioners might spring up from the ground at any moment; so that it became necessary, at any cost, to attempt to establish countermines to prevent this subterranean peril. One day, toward noon, two terrible detonations, which brought on a regular tornado of plaster and dust, shook the French legation, half burying under rubbish the lieutenant in command of the defences and several of his marines. But this was not all; all but two succeeded in getting clear of the stones and ashes that covered them to the shoulders, but two brave sailors never appeared again. And so the struggle continued, desperately, and under conditions more and more frightful.

And still the gentle stranger remained, when she might so easily have taken shelter elsewhere, — at the English legation, for instance, where most of the ministers with their families had found refuge; the balls did not penetrate to them; they were at the centre of the quarter defended by a few handfuls of brave soldiers, and could there feel a certain security so long as the barricades held out. But no, she remained and continued in her admirable role at that blazing point, the French legation, — a point which was the key, the cornerstone of the European quadrangle, whose capture would bring about general disaster.

One time they saw with their field glasses the posting of an imperial edict commanding that the fire against foreigners cease. (What they did *not* see was that the men who put up the notices were attacked by the crowd with knives.) Yet a certain lull, a sort of armistice did follow; the attacks became less violent.

They saw that incendiaries were everywhere abroad; they

heard fusillades, cannonades, and prolonged cries among the Chinese; entire districts were in flames; they were killing one another; their fury was fermenting as in a pandemonium, and they were suffocated, stifled with the smell of corpses.

Spies came occasionally with information to sell — always false and contradictory — in regard to the relief expedition, which amid ever-increasing anxiety was hourly expected. "It is here, it is there, it is advancing," or "It has been defeated and is retreating," were the announcements, yet it persisted in not appearing.

What, then, was Europe doing? Had they been abandoned? They continued, almost without hope, to defend themselves in their restricted quarters. Each day they felt that Chinese torture and death were closing in upon them.

They began to lack for the essentials of life. It was necessary to economize in everything, particularly in ammunition; they were growing savage, — when they captured any Boxers, instead of shooting them they broke their skulls with a revolver.

One day their ears, sharpened for all outside noises, distinguished a continued deep, heavy cannonade beyond the great black ramparts whose battlements were visible in the distance, and which enclosed them in a Dantesque circle; Pekin was being bombarded! It could only be by the armies of Europe come to their assistance.

Yet one last fear troubled their joy. Would not a supreme attack against them be attempted, an effort be made to destroy them before the allied troops could enter?

As a matter of fact they were furiously attacked, and this last day, the day of their deliverance, cost the life of one of our officers, Captain Labrousse, who went to join the Austrian commander in the glorious little cemetery of the legation. But they kept up their resistance, until all at once not a Chinese head was visible on the barricades of the enemy; all was empty and silent in the devastation about them; the Boxers were flying and the Allies were entering the city!

This first night of my arrival in Pekin was as melancholy as the nights on the road, but in a more commonplace way, with more of *ennui*. The workmen had just finished the walls of my room; the fresh plaster gave forth a chilling dampness that penetrated to my very bones, and as the room was empty, my servant spread my narrow mattress from the junk upon the floor, and began to make a table out of some old boxes.

My hosts were good enough to have a stove hastily set up for me and lighted, which called up a picture of European discomfort in some wretched place in the country. How could one fancy oneself in China, in Pekin itself, so near to mysterious enclosures, to palaces so full of wonders?

As to the French minister, whom I am anxious to see, to convey to him the admiral's communications, I learn that he, having no roof to cover his head, has gone to seek shelter at the Spanish legation; and furthermore, that he has typhoid fever, which is epidemic on account of the poisonous condition of the water, so that for the present no one can see him. So my stay in this damp place threatens to be more prolonged than I anticipated. Through the window-panes covered with moisture I gloomily look out onto a court filled with broken furniture, where the twilight is falling and the snow.

Who could have foreseen that to-morrow, by an unexpected turn of fortune, I should be sleeping on a great gilded, imperial bed in a strange fairyland in the heart of the Forbidden City?

VIII

FRIDAY, October 19.

I AWAKE BENUMBED with the damp cold of my poor lodging; water drips down the walls and the stove smokes.

I go off to perform a commission entrusted to me by the admiral for the commander-in-chief of our land troops, General Voyron, who lives in a small house near by. In the division of the mysterious Yellow City, made by the heads of the allied troops, one of the palaces of the Empress fell to our general. He installed himself there for the winter, not far from the palace which was to be occupied by one of our allies, Field-Marshal von Waldersee, and there he has graciously offered me hospitality. He himself leaves for Tien-Tsin to-day, so for the week or two which his trip will occupy I shall be there alone with his aide-de-camp, one of my old comrades, who has charge of adapting this residence from fairyland to the needs of military service.

What a change it will be from my plastered walls and charcoal stove!

My flight to the Yellow City will not take place till to-morrow morning, for my friend, the aide-de-camp, expresses his kindly wish to arrive before me at our palace, where some confusion reigns, and to prepare the place for me.

So, having no further duties to-day, I accept the offer of one of the members of the French legation to go with him to see the Temple of Heaven. It has stopped snowing, the cold north wind has chased away the clouds, and the sun is shining resplendently in the pale blue sky.

According to the map of Pekin, this Temple of Heaven is five or six kilometres from here, and is the largest of all the temples. It seems that it is situated in the midst of a park of venerable trees surrounded by double walls. Up to the time of the war the spot was unapproachable; the emperors came once a year and shut themselves up there for a solemn sacrifice, preceded by purifications and preparatory rites.

To reach it we have to go outside of all the ashes and ruins, outside of the Tartar City where we are staying, through the gigantic gates of the terrible walls, and penetrate to the Chinese City itself.

These two walled cities, which together make up Pekin, are two immense quadrilaterals placed side by side; one, the Tartar City, contains in a fortress-like enclosure the Yellow City, where I go to-morrow to take up my abode.

As we come through the separating wall and see the Chinese City framed by the colossal gateway, we are surprised to find a great artery, stately and full of life as in the old days, running straight through Pekin, which up to this time had seemed like a necropolis to us; the gold decorations, the color, the thousand forms of monsters were all unexpected, as well as the sudden aggression of noises, of music, and voices. This life, this agitation, this Chinese splendor, are inconceivable, inexplicable to us; such an abyss of dissimilarity lies between this world and ours!

The great artery stretches on before us broad and straight, — a road three or four kilometres long, leading finally to another monumental gate which appears in the distance, surmounted by a dungeon with an absurd roof. This is an opening through a wall beyond which is the outside solitude. The low houses which line the street on both sides seem to be made of gold lace, from top to bottom the open woodwork of their façades glitters; they are finely carved at the top, all shining with gold, with gargoyles similar to our own, and rows of gilded dragons. Black stele covered with gold letters rise much higher than the houses, from which jut out black and gold lacquered platforms for the support of strange emblems with horns and claws and monsters' faces.

Through the clouds of dust, the gilding, the dragons, and the chimæras glisten in the dusty sunlight as far as one can see. Above it all triumphal arches of astonishing lightness mount heavenward across the avenue; they are airy things of carved

wood, with supports like the masts of a ship, which repeat against the pale blue ether more strange hostile forms, horns, claws, and fantastic beasts.

On the broad highway where one treads as upon ashes, there is a dull rumbling of caravans and horses. The stupendous Mongolian camels, brown and woolly, attached to one another in long endless files, pass slowly and solemnly along, unceasingly like the waters of a river, raising as they walk the powdery bed which stifles the sounds of this entire city. They are going, who knows where, into the depths of the Thibetan or Mongolian deserts, carrying in the same indefatigable and unconscious way thousands of bales of merchandise; taking the place of canals and rivers which convey barges and junks over immense distances. So heavy is the dust raised by their feet that they can scarcely lift them; the legs of these innumerable camels in procession, as well as the lower parts of the houses, and the garments of the passers-by, are all vague and confused in outline, as though seen through the thick smoke of a forge, or through a shower of dark wool; but the backs of the great beasts with their shaggy coats, emerging from the soft clouds near the earth, are almost sharply defined, and the gold of the facades, tarnished below, shines brightly at the height of the extravagant cornices.

It seems like a phantasmagoric city with no real foundations, resting upon a cloud, a heavy cloud, whereon gigantic sheep, with necks enlarged by a thick brown fleece, move inoffensively.

Above the dust the sun shines clear and white, making resplendent the cold, penetrating light in which things stand out incisively. Objects that are high up above the ground stand out with absolute clearness. The smallest of small monsters on the top of the triumphal arches may be clearly seen, as well as the most delicate carving on the summits of the stele; one can even count the teeth, the forked tongues, the squinting eyes of the hundreds of gold chimæras which jut from the roofs.

Pekin, the city of carvings and gildings, the city of claws and horns, is still capable of creating illusions; on dry, sunny, windy days it recovers something of its splendor under the dust of the steppes, under the veil which then masks the shabbiness of its streets and the squalor of its crowds.

Yet all is old and worn in spite of the gilding which still remains bright. In this quarter there was continual fighting during the siege of the legations, the Boxers destroying the homes of those whom they suspected of sympathy for the barbarians.

The long avenue which we have been following for half an hour ends now at an arched bridge of white marble, still a superb object; here the houses come to an end, and on the opposite bank the gloomy steppes begin.

This was the Bridge of the Beggars, — dangerous inhabitants, who, before the capture of Pekin, ranged themselves on both sides of its long railing and extorted money from the passers-by; they formed a bold corporation with a king at its head, who often went armed. Their place is unoccupied to-day; the vagrants departed after the battles and massacres began.

Beyond this bridge a gray plain, empty and desolate, extends for two kilometres, as far as the Great Wall, far beyond where Pekin ends. The road, with its tide of caravans, goes straight on through this solitude to the outside gate. Why should this desert be enclosed by the city's walls? There is not a trace of previous constructions; it must always have been as it is. No one is in sight on it; a few stray dogs, a few rags, a few bones, and that is all.

For a long distance into this steppe there are sombre red walls at both right and left which seem to enclose great cedar woods. The enclosure at the right is that of the Temple of Agriculture; at the left is the Temple of Heaven, for which we are bound. We plunge into this gloomy region, leaving the dust and the crowds behind.

The enclosure around the Temple of Heaven has a circumference of more than six kilometres; it is one of the most extensive in the whole city, where everything is on an old-time scale of grandeur which overpowers us to-day. The gate which was formerly impassable will not close now, and we enter the wood of venerable trees — cedars, arbor vitæ, and willows — through which long avenues have been cut. This spot, accustomed to silence and respect, is now profaned by barbarian cavalry. Several thousand Indians sent out to China by England are encamped there; their horses have trampled the grass; the turf and the moss are filled with rubbish and manure. From a marble terrace where incense to the gods was formerly burned, clouds of infected smoke were rising, the English having chosen this place for the burning of cattle that die of the plague, and for the manufacture of bone-black.

There are, as in all sacred woods, two enclosures. The secondary temples, scattered amongst the cedars, precede the great central temple.

Never having been here before, we are guided by our judgment toward something which must be it, higher than anything else, above the tops of the trees, — a distant rotunda with a roof of blue enamel, surmounted by a gold sphere which glistens in the sunshine.

The rotunda, when we finally reach it, proves to be the sanctuary itself. Its approaches are silent; there are no more horses or barbarian riders. It stands on a high esplanade of white marble reached by a series of steps and by an "imperial path," reserved for the Son of Heaven, who is not permitted to mount stairs. An "imperial path" is an inclined plane, usually an enormous monolith of marble placed at an easy angle, upon which the five-clawed dragon is sculptured in bas-relief; the scales of the great heraldic animal, its coils and its nails, serve to sustain the Emperor's steps and to prevent his feet, dressed in silk, from slipping on the strange path reserved for Him alone, and which no Chinese would dare to tread.

We mount irreverently by this "imperial path," scratching the fine white scales of the dragon with our coarse shoes.

From the top of the lonely terrace, melancholy and everlastingly white with the unchanging whiteness of marble, one sees above the trees of the wood, great Pekin in its dust, which the sun is beginning to gild as it gilds the tiny evening clouds.

The gate of the temple is open, and guarded by an Indian trooper with oblong sphynx-like eyes, as out of his element as we in this ultra-Chinese and sacred environment. He salutes us and permits us to enter.

The circular temple is bright with red and gold and has a roof of blue enamel; it is a new temple built to replace a very old one which was burned ten years ago. The altar is bare, it is bare everywhere; plunderers have passed over it, leaving nothing but the marble pavements, the beautiful lacquered ceilings, and the walls; the tall columns of red lacquer, arranged in the form of a circle, all taper uniformly and are decorated with garlands of gold flowers.

On the esplanade around it, weeds have pushed their way here and there between the carved stones of the pavement, attesting the extreme age of the marble in spite of its immaculate whiteness. It is a commanding place, erected at great expense for the contemplation of the sovereigns, and we linger, like the Sons of Heaven themselves, to gaze upon it.

In our immediate vicinity the tops of the arbor-vitæ and the cedars, — the great wood which envelops us in calm and silence, — come first. Then, toward the north is the endless but obscure

city, which seems almost unreal; one divines rather than sees it, so hidden is it in the smoke or fog which forms a gauzy veil. It might be a mirage were it not for the monumental roofs of exaggerated proportions, whose tops of shining enamel emerge from the fog here and there, clear and real; these are palaces and pagodas. Beyond all this, very far away, is the crest of the mountains of Mongolia, which to-night have no base and seem to be cut out of blue and red paper high up in the air. Toward the west is the gray steppe through which we have come; the slow procession of caravans crossing it marks upon it as far as the eye can see an uninterrupted brown path; we realize that this endless procession goes on for hundreds of miles, and that on all the great roads of China, to its most distant frontiers, similar processions are moving with identical slowness.

It is the old unchanging method of communication between these men so different from ourselves, — men with perseverance and infinite patience, for whom the march of time, which unsteadies us, does not exist; it forms for them the arterial circulation of this boundless empire, where four or five hundred million brains — the reverse of our own and forever incomprehensible to us — live and speculate.

Chapter IV

In the Imperial City

I

SATURDAY, October 20.

IT SNOWS. The sky is lowering and overcast, with no hope of clearing, as though there were no longer any sun. A furious north wind is blowing, and the black dust whirls and eddies, commingling with the snowflakes.

This morning, my first interview with our minister took place at the Spanish legation. His temperature has fallen, but he is still very weak, and must remain in bed for some days, so I am obliged to postpone until to-morrow or the day after the communications I have to make to him.

I take my last meal with the members of the French legation in the chancellor's house, where, in default of sumptuous quarters, they have offered me the most kindly hospitality. At half-past one the two little Chinese chariots arrive, lent me for the emigration of myself, my people, and my light luggage to the Yellow City.

The Chinese chariots are very small, very massive, very heavy, and entirely without springs; mine has something of the elegance of a hearse; the outside is covered with a slaty-gray silk, with a wide border of black velvet.

We are to journey toward the northwest, in the opposite direction from the Chinese City where we were yesterday, and from the Temple of Heaven. We have five or six kilometres to go almost at a walk, on account of the pitiable condition of the streets and bridges, where most of the paving stones are missing.

These Chinese chariots cannot be closed; they are like a simple sentry box mounted on wheels, — so to-day we are lashed by the wind, cut by the snow, blinded by the dust.

First come the ruins of the legation district, full of soldiers. Then more lonely, almost deserted and entirely Chinese ruins — one gray, dusty devastation, seen vaguely through clouds of black and clouds of white. At the gates and on the bridges are European or Japanese sentinels, for the whole city is under military rule. From time to time we meet soldiers and ambulances carrying the flag of the Red-Cross Society.

At last the first enclosure of the Yellow or Imperial City is announced by the interpreter of the French legation, who has kindly offered to be my guide, and to share my chariot with its funeral trappings. I try to look, but the wind burns my eyes.

We are passing with frightful jolts through great blood-colored ramparts, not by way of a gate, but through a breach made with a mine by Indian cavalrymen.

Pekin, on the farther side of this wall, is somewhat less injured. In some of the streets the houses have kept their outside covering of gilded woodwork and their rows of chimæras along the edges of the roofs; all this is crumbling and decayed, it is true, licked by the flames or riddled by grape-shot. An evil-looking rabble, dressed in sheepskins or blue cotton rags, still swarms in some of the houses.

Another rampart of the same blood red and a great gate ornamented with faience through which we must pass, — this time it is the real gate of the Imperial City, the gate of the region which no one was ever allowed to enter; it is to me as though it had been announced as the gate to mystery or to an enchanted land.

We enter, and my surprise is great; for it is not a city, but a wood, — a sombre wood, infested with crows which croak in the gray branches. The trees are the same as those at the Temple of Heaven, — cedars, arbor-vitæ, and willows, — old trees all of them, of twisted shapes, unknown in our country. Sleet and snow cling to their branches, and the inevitable dust in the narrow, windy paths engulfs us.

There are also wooded hills where kiosks of faience rise among the cedars; in spite of their height, it is plain that they are artificial. Obscured by the snow and dust, we can see here and there in the distant wood austere old palaces, with enamelled roofs, guarded by horrible marble monsters which crouch at the thresholds.

The whole place is of an incontestable beauty, while at the same time it is dismal, unfriendly, and disturbing under this sombre sky.

Now we approach some enormous object which we shall soon be alongside of. Is it a fortress, a prison, or something more lugubrious still? Double ramparts without end, always blood red, with gloomy dungeons and a moat thirty metres wide, full of water-lilies and dying roses. This is the Violet City, enclosed in the heart of the impenetrable Imperial City, and more impenetrable still. It is the residence of the Invisible, of the Son of Heaven — God! but the place is gloomy, hostile, savage, beneath this sombre sky!

We continue to advance under the old trees into what seems the park of death.

These dumb, closed palaces, seen first on one side, then on the other, are the Temple of the God of the Clouds, the Temple of Imperial Longevity, or the Temple of the Benediction of Sacred Mountains. Their names, inconceivable to us, the names of an Asiatic dream, make them still more unreal.

My companion assures me that this Yellow City is not always so terrible as it is to-day; for this weather is exceptional in a

Chinese autumn, which is usually magnificently luminous. He promises me afternoons of warm sunshine in this wood, unique in all the world, where I shall make my home for several days.

"Now look," he said, "look! This is the Lake of the Lotus, and that is the Marble Bridge."

The Lake of the Lotus and the Marble Bridge! These two names have long been known to me as the names of things *which could not be seen*, but of things whose reputations had crossed insurmountable walls. They call up images of light and intense color, and are a surprise to me here in this mournful desert, in this icy wind.

The Lake of the Lotus! I had pictured it as sung by the Chinese poets, of an exquisite limpidity with great calices open to an abundance of water, a sort of aquatic plain covered with pink flowers, pink from one end to the other. And this is it! — This slime and this gloomy swamp, covered with dead leaves turned brown by the frost! It is infinitely larger than I supposed, this lake made by the hand of man; it goes on and on toward nostalgic shores, where ancient pagodas appear among the old trees, under the gray sky.

The Marble Bridge! Yes, this long, white arch supported by a series of white pillars, this exceedingly graceful curve, the balustrades with monsters' heads, — this all corresponds to the idea I had of it; it is very sumptuous and very Chinese. I had not, however, foreseen the two dead bodies decaying in their robes, which lay among the reeds at the entrance to the bridge.

The large dead leaves on the lake are really lotus-leaves; I recognize them now that I see them near at hand, and remember to have seen similar ones — but oh, so green and fresh — on the ponds of Nagasaki or of Yeddo. And there once must have been here the effect of an uninterrupted covering of pink blossoms; their fading stems rise now by thousands above the slime.

They will undoubtedly die, these fields of lotus, which for centuries have charmed the eyes of the emperors, for the lake is almost empty; it is the Allies who have turned its water into the canal that connects Pekin with the river, in order to re-establish this route which the Chinese had dried up for fear of its serving the purpose of the invaders.

The Marble Bridge, white and solitary, leads us across to the other bank of the lake, very narrow at this point, and there I shall find the Palace of the North, which is to be my residence. At first I do not see that there are enclosures within enclosures, all with great gates, dilapidated and in ruins. A dull light falls from the wintry sky through opaque clouds that are filled with snow.

In the centre of a gray wall there is a breach where an African chasseur is on guard; on one side lies a dead dog, on the other a pile of rags and filth breathing a corpse-like odor. This, it appears, is the entrance to my palace.

We are black with dust, powdered with snow, and our teeth are chattering with cold, when we finally get down from our chariot in a court encumbered with débris, where my comrade, Captain C., the aide-de-camp, comes to meet me. With an approach like this, one well might wonder if the promised palace were not chimerical.

Just back of this court there is, however, the first appearance of magnificence. Here and there is a long gallery of glass, light, elegant, and apparently intact, amid so much destruction. Through the panes one has glimpses of gold, porcelains, and imperial silks with designs of dragons and clouds. This is one corner of the palace, completely hidden until you are right upon it.

Oh, our evening meal on the night of our arrival in this strange dwelling! It is almost totally dark. At an ebony table my companion and I are seated, wrapped in our military cloaks with collars turned up, our teeth chattering with cold, and are served by our orderlies with trembling limbs. A feeble little Chinese candle of red wax, stuck in a bottle, — a candle picked up in the débris from some ancestral altar, — sheds a dim light, blown as it is by the wind. Our plates, in fact all the dishes, are of porcelain of inestimable value, — imperial yellow, marked with the cipher of a fastidious emperor, who was a contemporary of Louis XV. But our wine and our muddy water — boiled and reboiled for fear of poison in the wells — are in horrible old bottles with bits of potato, cut into shape by the soldiers, for corks.

The gallery where this scene takes place is very long; the distance is lost in obscurity where the splendors of an Asiatic tale are dimly perceived. Its sides are of glass up to the height of a man, and this frail wall is all that separates us from the sinister darkness which surrounds us; one has a feeling that the wandering forms outside, the phantoms attracted by our small light, may from a distance see us at table, and this is disturbing. Above the glass there is a series of light frames containing rice-paper, which reach to the ceiling, from which marvellous ebony sculptures depend, delicate as lacework; this rice-paper is torn, and allows the mortally cold night wind to strike us. Our frozen feet rest on imperial yellow carpets of the finest wool, with the five-horned dragons sprawling upon them. Close to us gigantic incense-burners of cloisonné of the old inimitable blue, with gold elephants as pedestals, are softly burning; there are magnificent and fanciful screens; phœnixes of enamel spread their long wings; thrones, monsters, things without age and without price abound. And there we are, inelegant, dusty, worn, soiled, with the air of coarse barbarians, installed like intruders in fairyland.

What must this gallery have been scarcely three months ago, when instead of silence and death there was life, music, and flowers; when a crowd of courtiers and servants in silken robes peopled these approaches so empty and ruined to-day; when the Empress, followed by the ladies of the palace, passed by dressed like goddesses!

Having finished our supper, which consisted of the regular army ration, having finished drinking our tea out of museum-like porcelain, now for the hour of smoking and conversation. No, we try in vain to think it amusing to be here, in this unforeseen and half fantastic way. It is too cold; the wind chills us to the marrow. We do not enjoy anything. We prefer to go off and to try to sleep.

My comrade, Captain C., who has taken possession of the place, leads me with a lantern and a few followers to the apartment set aside for me. It is on the *rez-de-chausée*, of course; there are no real stories in Chinese houses. As in the gallery, from which we come, there is nothing between me and the night outside but a few panes of glass, very light shades of white silk, and windows of rice-paper torn from one end to the other. As to the door, which is made of one great panel of glass, I fasten it with a cord, since there is no lock.

There are some admirable yellow rugs on the floor, thick as cushions. I have a big imperial bed of carved ebony, and my mattress and pillows are covered with precious silk embroidered in gold, but there are no sheets, although I have a soldier's gray woollen blanket.

To-morrow my companion tells me I may go and select from her Majesty's reserve supply whatever I wish in the way of further decorations for this room, as it can do no one any harm to move things about.

Assuring me that the gates of the outer enclosure, as well as the breach by which I entered, are guarded by sentinels, he retires with his orderlies to the other end of the palace.

Dressed, and with my boots on, I stretch myself out on the beautiful silk cushions, adding to my gray blanket an old sheepskin and two or three imperial robes embroidered with gold chimæras. My two servants arrange themselves in like manner on the floor. Before blowing out the red candle from some ancestral altar, I am constrained to admit in my secret soul that the accusation that we are "Occidental barbarians" has been completely confirmed since supper.

The wind has tormented and torn all that was left of the rice-paper in my panes; above me there is a perpetual sound like the movement of the wings of nocturnal birds or the flight of bats. I distinguish occasionally, although half asleep, a short fusillade or an isolated cry in the distance.

II

SUNDAY, October 21.

Cold, darkness, death, all that oppressed us last night, has disappeared with the morning light. The sun shines warm as a summer sun. The somewhat disordered Chinese magnificence which surrounds us is bright with the light of the East.

It is amusing to go on a voyage of discovery over this almost hidden palace, which lurks in a low spot, behind walls, under trees, looking quite insignificant as you approach it, but is, together with its dependencies, almost as large as a city.

It is made up of long galleries enclosed on all sides in glass; the light framework, the verandahs, the small columns, are painted on the outside a greenish bronze decorated with pink water-lilies.

One has the feeling that it was built according to the fancies of a woman; it even seems as though the splendid old Empress had left in it, along with her bibelots, a touch of her superannuated yet still charming grace.

The galleries cross one another at right angles, forming courts at the junctures, like little cloisters. They are filled with objects of art, which can be equally well seen from without, for the entire palace is transparent from one end to the other. There is nothing to protect all this glass even at night; the place was enclosed by so many walls and seemed so inviolable that no other precaution was deemed necessary.

Within, the architectural elegance consists of arches of rare wood, crossing at frequent intervals; they are made of enormous beams so carved, so leafy, so open, that they seem like lace, or, rather, like bowers of dark leaves that form a perspective comparable to the lanes in old parks.

The wing which we occupy must have been the wing of honor. The farther away from it one goes in the direction of the woods where the palace ends, the more simple does the decoration become. At one end are the lodgings of the mandarins, the stewards, the gardeners, the domestics, all hurriedly abandoned and full of unfamiliar objects, household utensils or those used in worship, ceremonial hats and court liveries.

Then comes an enclosed garden which is entered by an elaborately carved marble gate. Here one finds small fountains, pretentious and curious rockwork, and rows of vases containing plants which have died from lack of water or from cold. Further on there is an orchard where figs, grapes, eggplant, pumpkins, and gourds were cultivated, — gourds especially, for in China they are emblems of happiness, and it was the custom of the Empress to offer one with her own white hands to each of the dignitaries who came to pay his court to her in exchange for the magnificent presents he brought her. There are also small pavilions for the cultivation of silkworms and little kiosks for storing edible grains; each kind was kept in a porcelain jar decorated with imperial dragons, worthy of a place in a museum.

The parks of this artificial little landscape end in the brush, where they lose themselves under the leafless trees of the wood where to-day the crows and the magpies are enjoying the beautiful autumn sun. It seems that when the Empress gave up the regency — and we know by what an audacious manœuvre she so quickly managed to take it up again — it was her caprice to construct a bit of the country here in the heart of Pekin, in the very centre of this immense human ant-hill.

The most surprising thing in all this enclosure is a Gothic church with two granite bell-towers, a parsonage, and a school, — all built in other days by the missionaries and all of enormous size. But in order to create this palace it was necessary to enlarge the limits of the Imperial City and to include in them this Christian territory; so the Empress gave the Lazarist Fathers more land and a more beautiful church, erected at her own expense, where the missionaries and several thousand converts endured all last summer the horrors of a four-months' siege.

Like the systematic woman that she was, her Majesty utilized the church and its dependencies for storing her reserves of all sorts, packed in innumerable boxes. One could not imagine without having seen them what an accumulation there could be of the strange, the marvellous, and the preposterous in the reserve stock of bibelots belonging to an Empress of China.

The Japanese were the first to forage there, then came the Cossacks, and, lastly, the Germans, who left the place to us. At present the church is in indescribable disorder, — boxes opened, their precious contents scattered outside in rubbish heaps; there are streams of broken china, cascades of enamel, ivory, and porcelain.

In the long glass galleries a similar state of things exists. My comrade, who is charged with straightening out the chaos and making an inventory, reminds me of that person who was shut up by an evil spirit in a chamber filled with the feathers of all the birds of the woods and compelled to sort them by species; those of the finch, the linnet, the bullfinch together. However, he has already set about his difficult task, and with Chinese workmen, under the direction of a few marines and some African chasseurs, has already begun to clear things away.

Five metres from here, on the opposite shores of the Lake of the Lotus, as I was retracing my steps last night, I found a second palace which once belonged to the Empress, which is now ours also. In this palace, which no one is occupying at the moment, I am authorized to set up my work-room for a few days, so that I may have quiet and isolation.

It is called the Rotunda Palace. Exactly opposite the Marble Bridge, it resembles a circular fortress, on which have been placed small miradors, − little, fairy-like castles, − and the single low entrance is guarded day and night by soldiers, whose orders are to admit no one.

When you have crossed the threshold of this citadel, and the guards have closed the door after you, you penetrate into the most exquisite solitude. An inclined plane leads you to a vast esplanade about twelve metres above the ground, where the miradors − the little kiosks − seen from below stand; there is a garden with old, old trees, a labyrinth of rocks, and a large pagoda shining with gold and enamel.

From here there is a commanding view of the palace and its park. On one side the Lake of the Lotus is spread out; on the other, one has a bird's-eye view of the Violet City, showing the almost endless succession of high imperial roofs, − a world of roofs, a world of enamel shining in the sunshine, a world of horns, claws, and monsters on gable and tiling.

I walk in the solitude of this high place, in the shade of the old trees, trying to understand the arrangement of the house and to choose a study to my fancy.

In the centre of the esplanade is the magnificent pagoda

which was struck by a shell and which is still in battle disarray. Its presiding divinity — a white goddess, who was the Palladium of the Chinese empire, an alabaster goddess with a gold dress embroidered with precious stones — meditates with downcast eyes, sweet, calm, and smiling, in the midst of the destruction of her sacred vases, of her incense-burners and her flowers.

One large gloomy room has kept its furnishings intact, — an admirable ebony throne, some screens, seats of all shapes, and cushions of heavy yellow imperial silk, brocaded with a cloud effect.

Among all the silent kiosks the one which I fix upon as my choice is at the very edge of the esplanade on the crest of the surrounding wall, overlooking the Lake of the Lotus and the Marble Bridge, and commanding a view of the whole factitious landscape, — created out of gold ingots and human lives to please the weary eyes of emperors.

It is hardly larger than a ship's cabin, but its sides are made of glass extending to the roof, so that I shall be kept warm until nightfall by the autumn sun, which here in China is seldom overclouded. I have a table and two ebony chairs with yellow silk coverings brought in from the adjoining room, — and thus installed, I descend again to the Marble Bridge and return to the Palace of the North, where Captain C., my companion in this Chinese dream, is waiting breakfast for me.

I arrive in time to see, before they are burned, the curious discoveries of the morning, — the decorations, emblems, and accessories of the Chinese Imperial Theatre. They were cumbersome, frail things, intended to serve but for a night or two, and then forgotten for an indefinite time in a room that was never opened, and which they are now clearing out and cleaning for a hospital for our sick and wounded. Mythological representations were evidently given at this theatre, the scene taking place either in hell or with the gods in the clouds; and such a collection as there was of monsters, chimæras, wild beasts, and devils, in cardboard or paper, mounted on carcasses made of bamboo or whalebone, all devised with a perfect genius for the horrible, with an imagination surpassing the limits of a nightmare!

The rats, the dampness, and the ants have caused irremediable havoc among them, so it has been decided to burn all these figures that have served to amuse or to trouble the dreams of the drowsy, dissipated, feeble young Emperor.

Our soldiers are hurrying amid joy and laughter to carry all these things out of doors. Here in the morning sunlight of the courtyard are apocalyptic beasts and life-sized elephants that weigh nothing at all, and which one man can make walk or run. They kick them, they jump upon them, they jump into them, they walk through them and reduce them to nothing; then at last they light the gay torch, which in the twinkling of an eye consumes them.

Other soldiers have been working all the morning pasting rice-paper into the sashes of our palace so that the wind shall not enter. As for artificial heat, it comes up from below, Chinese fashion, from subterranean furnaces which are arranged under the rooms, and which we shall light this evening as soon as the chill comes on. For the moment the splendid sunshine suffices; so much glass in the galleries, where the silks, enamels, and gold glisten, gives us the heat of a greenhouse, and on this occasion we take our meal, which is always served on the Emperor's china, in an illusion of summer.

The sky of Pekin is subject to excessive and sudden variations of which we with our regular climate can form no conception. Toward the middle of the day, when I find myself out of doors again under the cedars of the Yellow City, the sun has suddenly disappeared behind some leaden clouds which seem heavy with snow; the Mongolian wind begins to blow, bitter cold, as it was yesterday, and again a northern winter follows with no transition stage a few hours of the radiant weather of the *Midi*.

I have an arrangement to meet the members of the French legation in the woods, to explore with them the sepulchral Violet City, which is the centre, the heart, the mystery of China, the veritable abode of the Son of Heaven, the enormous Sardanapalian citadel, in comparison with which all the small modern palaces in the Imperial City where we are living seem but children's playthings.

Even since the flight it has not been easy to enter the Violet City with its yellow enamelled roofs. Behind the double walls, mandarins and eunuchs still dwell in this home of magnificence and oppression, and it is said that a few women, hidden princesses, and treasures still remain. The two gates are guarded by severe sentries, — the north gate by the Japanese, the south by Americans.

It is by the first of these two entrances that we are authorized to pass to-day, and the group of small Japanese soldiers that we find there smile upon us in welcome; but the austere gate — dark red with gilded locks and hinges, representing the heads of monsters — is closed from within and resists their efforts. The use of centuries has warped the enormous doors so that through the crack one can see boards fastened on to the inside to prevent their opening, and persons running about announcing in flute-like voices that they have received no orders.

We threaten to burn the doors, to climb over them, to shoot through the opening; all sorts of things which we have no intention of doing, but which frighten the eunuchs and put them to flight.

No one is left to answer us. What are we to do? We are freezing our feet by this cold wall; the moat, full of dead reeds, exhales dampness, and the wind continues to blow.

The kindly Japanese, however, send some of their strongest men — who depart on a keen run — to the other gate, some four kilometres around. They light a fire for us out of cedar branches and painted woodwork, where we take turns warming our hands while we wait; we amuse ourselves by picking up here and there old feathered arrows thrown by prince or emperor from the top of the walls. After an hour's patient waiting, noise and voices are heard behind the silent gate; it is our envoy inside cuffing the eunuchs.

Suddenly the boards creak and fall and the doors open wide before us.

III

THE ABANDONED ROOM

THERE IS A faint odor of tea in the dark room, an odor of I know not what beside, — of dried flowers and old silks.

There is no way of getting more light in this curious room, which opens into a big gloomy salon, for its windows receive only half-light because of the rice paper in all the panes; they open onto a yard that is no doubt surrounded by triple walls. The alcove-bed, large and low, which seems to be set into an inner wall thick as a rampart, has silk curtains and a cover of dark blue, — the color of the sky at night. There are no seats, indeed there would scarcely be room for any; neither are there any books, nor could one very well see to read. On the dark wooden chests which serve as tables, stand melancholy bibelots in glass cases; small vases of bronze or of jade containing very stiff artificial bouquets, with petals made of mother-of-pearl and ivory. A thick layer of dust over everything shows that the room is not occupied.

At first sight there is nothing to mark the place or the time, —
unless, possibly, the fineness of the ebony carving of the upper
part of the bed reveals the patience of the Chinese. Everything is
sombre and gloomy, with straight, austere lines.

Where are we, then, in what obscure, closed, clandestine
dwelling?

Has some one lived here in our time or was it in the distant
past?

How many hours — or how many centuries — has he
been gone, and who could he have been, the occupant of the
abandoned room?

Some sad dreamer evidently, to have chosen this shadowy
retreat; some one very refined, to have left behind him this
distinguished fragrance, and very weary, to have been pleased
with this dull simplicity and this eternal twilight.

One feels stifled by the smallness of the windows, whose
panes are veiled with silky paper, and which never can be opened
to admit light or air because they are sealed into the wall. And
besides, you recall the weary way you must take to get here, and
the obstacles you encounter, and that disturbs you.

First, there is the big black Babylonian wall, the superhuman
ramparts of a city more than ten leagues around, which to-day
is a mass of ruins, half empty, and strewn with corpses; then
a second wall, painted blood-red, which forms a second city
enclosed in the first. Then a third wall, more magnificent still, and
also the color of blood; this is the wall that surrounds the great
mysteries of the place, and before the days of the war and the
fall of the city no European had ever gone beyond it; to-day we
were detained for more than an hour, in spite of passes, signed
and countersigned; through the keyhole of a great gate guarded
by soldiers and barricaded from within, we were compelled
to threaten and argue at length with the guards inside, who

sought to hide and to escape. These gates once opened, another wall appeared, separated from the former one by a road going all the way around the enclosure; here tattered garments were scattered about, and dogs were playing with the bones of the dead. This wall was of the same red, but still more splendid, and was crowned along its entire length by a horned ornamentation and by monsters made of a golden yellow faience. When we had finally passed this third wall, queer old beardless persons came to meet us with distrustful greetings, and guided us through a maze of little courts and small gardens, walled and walled again, in which old trees were growing amongst rock-work and jars. All of it was separate, concealed, distressing; all of it protected and peopled by monsters and chimæras in bronze or marble, by a thousand faces, whose grimaces signified ferocity and hatred, by a thousand unknown symbols. And every time each gate in the red walls with the yellow faience tops closed behind us, as in horrible dreams the doors of a series of passageways close upon one, nevermore to permit one to go out.

Now, after our long journey which seems like a nightmare, we feel, as we look at the anxious group who have conducted us, walking noiselessly on their paper soles, that we have committed some supreme and unheard-of profanation in their eyes, in penetrating to this modest room; they stand there in the doorway, peering obliquely at our every gesture; the crafty eunuchs in silken robes, and the thin mandarins, wearing along with the red button of their headdresses, the melancholy raven's quill. They were compelled to yield, they did not wish to; they tried by every ruse to lead us to some other part of the immense labyrinth of this palace of Heliogabalus; to interest us in the luxurious salons farther on, in the great courts, and in the marble balconies, which we shall see later; in a whole Versailles some distance farther on, now overgrown by weeds, and where no sound is heard but the song of the crows.

They were determined we should not come here, and it was by observing the dilation of the pupils of their frightened eyes that we guessed which way to go.

Who lived here, then, sequestered behind so many walls, — walls more terrible by far than those of our western prisons? Who could he have been, the man who slept in this bed under these silken covers of nocturnal blue, and in his times of revery, at nightfall or at dawn, on glacial winter days, was obliged to contemplate these pensive little bouquets under glass, ranged so symmetrically along the black chests?

It was he, the invisible Emperor, Son of Heaven, childish and feeble; he whose empire is vaster than all Europe, and who reigns like a vague phantom over four or five hundred millions of subjects.

It is the same person in whose veins the vigor of half-deified ancestors is exhausted, who has too long remained inactive, concealed in this palace more sacred than a temple; the same who neglects and envelops in twilight the diminishing place where he is pleased to live. The immense setting in which former emperors lived frightens him and he abandons it all; grass and brushwood grow on the majestic marble railings and in the grand courtyards; crows and pigeons by the hundreds make their nests in the gilded vaults of the throne room, covering with dirt and dung the rich and curious rugs left there to be ruined. This inviolable palace, a league in circumference, which no foreigner has ever seen, of which one can learn nothing, guess nothing, has in store for Europeans who enter it for the first time the surprise of mournful dilapidation and the silence of a tomb.

The pale Emperor never occupied the throne rooms. No, what suited him was the quarter where the small gardens were, and the enclosed yards, the quaint quarter where the eunuchs tried to prevent our going. The alcove-bed in its deep recess, with its curtains like the blue of night, indicates fear.

The small private apartments behind this gloomy chamber extend like subterranean passages into still deeper shadows; ebony is the prevailing wood; everything is intentionally sombre, even the mournful mummified bouquets under their glass cases. There is a soft-toned piano which the young Emperor was learning to play, in spite of his long, brittle nails; a harmonium, and a big music-box that gives Chinese airs with a tone that seems to come from beneath the waters of a lake.

Beyond this comes what was doubtless his most cherished retreat, — it is narrow and low like the cabin of a ship, and exhales the fine odor of tea and dried rose-leaves.

There, in front of a small airhole covered with rice paper, through which filters a little sombre light, lies a mattress, covered with imperial golden-yellow silk, which seems to retain the imprint of a body habitually extended upon it. A few books, a few private papers, are scattered about. Fastened to the wall are two or three unimportant pictures, not even framed, representing colorless roses, and written in Chinese characters underneath are the last orders of the physician for this chronic invalid.

What was the real character of this dreamer, who shall ever say? What distorted views of life had been bequeathed to him of the things of this world and of the world beyond? What do all these gruesome symbols signify to him? The emperors, the demigods, from whom he descends, made old Asia tremble; tributary sovereigns came from great distances to prostrate themselves, filling this place with banners and processions more magnificent than our imaginations can picture; within these same walls, so silent to-day, how and under what passing phantasmagoric aspects did he retain the stamp of the wonderful past?

And what confusion must have entered his unfathomable little brain when the unprecedented act was accomplished, and events occurred which he never in his wildest fears could have anticipated! His palace, with its triple walls, violated to its most secret recesses; he, the Son of Heaven, torn from the dwelling where twenty generations of his ancestors had lived inaccessible; obliged to flee, and in his flight to permit himself to be seen, to act in the light of day like other men, perhaps even to implore and to wait!

Just as we are leaving the abandoned room our orderlies, who purposely remained behind, laughingly throw themselves on the bed with the nocturnal blue curtains, and I hear one of them remark gaily in an aside and with a Gascon accent: " Now, old fellow, we can say that we have lain on the bed of the Emperor of China."

IV

MONDAY, October 22.

CHINESE WORKMEN, — amongst whom we are warned that there are spies and Boxers, — who look after the fires in the two furnaces in our palace, have kept us almost too warm all night. When we get up there is, as there was yesterday, another illusion of summer on our light verandah with the green columns painted with pink lotus flowers. An almost burning sun is rising and shining upon the ghostly pilgrimage which I am about to make on horseback, toward the west, outside the Tartar City, and through the ashy, silent, ruined suburbs.

In this direction there were, scattered through the dusty country, Christian cemeteries which even in 1860 had never been violated by the yellow race. But this time they furiously attacked the dead, and left chaos and abomination behind them. The oldest remains, those of missionaries who had been sleeping there for three centuries, were disinterred, crushed, piled up and set on fire in order to destroy, according to Chinese beliefs, whatever might still be left of their souls. One must be somewhat acquainted with the ideas of the country in order to understand the enormity of this supreme insult to all our Occidental races.

The cemetery of the Jesuit Fathers was singularly splendid. They were formerly very powerful with the Celestial Emperors, and borrowed for their own tombs the funereal emblems of the princes of China. The ground is literally strewn now with big marble dragons and tortoises, and with tall stele with chimæras coiled about them; all these carvings have been thrown down and smashed; the heavy stones of the vaults have been broken also, and the ground thoroughly overturned.

A more modest enclosure, not far away, has for a long time been the burial-place for the European legations. It has undergone the same treatment as the beautiful cemetery of the Jesuits. The Chinese have ransacked the graves, destroyed the bodies, and even violated the coffins of little children. Some few human bones are still lying on the ground, while the crosses that marked the graves are placed upside down. It is one of the most poignantly affecting sights that ever met my eyes.

Some good Sisters who lived near by kept a school for Chinese children; of their houses nothing is left but a pile of bricks and ashes, even the trees have been uprooted and stuck back in the ground head foremost.

This is their story: —

They were alone one night when about a thousand Boxers came along, shouting their death cries and playing gongs. The Sisters began to pray in their chapel as they awaited death. However, the noise died away, and when day broke no one was in sight, so they escaped to Pekin and took shelter with the bishop, taking their frightened little pupils with them. When the

Boxers were asked later why they had not entered and killed the Sisters, they replied: "Because we saw soldiers' heads and guns all around the convent walls." So the Sisters owed their lives to this hallucination of their executioners.

The wells in the deserted gardens fill the air to-day with odors of the dead. There were three large cisterns which furnished a water so pure that they sent all the way from the legations to get it. The Boxers filled these wells up to the brim with the mutilated bodies of little boys from the Brothers' school and from Christian families in the neighborhood. Dogs came to eat from the horrible pile which came up to the level of the ground; but they had their fill, and so the bodies were left, and have been so preserved by the cold and dryness that the marks of torture upon them may still be seen. One poor thigh has been slashed in stripes after the manner in which bakers sometimes mark their loaves of bread, another poor hand is without nails. And here is a woman from whom one of the private parts of her body has been cut and placed in her mouth, where it was left by the dogs between her gaping jaws. The bodies are covered with what looks like salt, but which proves to be white frost, which in shady places never melts here. Yet there is enough clear, implacable sunshine to bring out the emaciation and to exaggerate the horrors of the open mouths, their agonized expressions, and the rigidity of the anguished positions of the dead.

There is not a cloud to-day, but a pale sky which reflects a great deal of light. All winter, it seems, it is much the same; even in the coldest weather rains and snows are very exceptional in Pekin.

After our brief soldiers' breakfast, served on rare china in the long gallery, I leave the Palace of the North to install myself in the kiosk on the opposite shore, which I selected yesterday, and to begin my work. It is about two o'clock; a summer's sun shines on my solitary path, on the whiteness of the Marble Bridge, on the mud of the Lake, and on the bodies that sleep amongst the frosted lotus leaves.

The guards at the entrance to the Rotunda Palace open and close behind me the red lacquered doors. I mount the inclined plane leading to the esplanade, and here I am alone, much alone, in the silence of my lofty garden and my strange palace.

In order to reach my work-room, I have to go along narrow passageways between old trees and the most unnatural rockwork. The kiosk is flooded with light, the beautiful sunshine falls on my table and on my black seats with their cushions of golden yellow; the beautiful melancholy October sunshine illumines and warms my chosen retreat, where the Empress, it seems, loved to come and sit and watch from this high point her lake all pink with flowers.

The last butterflies and the last wasps, their lives prolonged by this hot-house warmth, beat their wings against the window-panes. The great imperial lake is spread out before us, spanned by the Marble Bridge; venerable trees form a girdle around shores out of which rise the fanciful roofs of palaces and pagodas, — roofs that are one marvellous mass of faience. As in the landscapes painted on Chinese fans, there are groups of tiny rocks in the foreground, and small enamelled monsters from a neighboring kiosk, while in the middle distance there are knotted branches which have fallen from some old cedar.

I am alone, entirely and deliciously alone, high up in an inaccessible spot whose approaches are guarded by sentinels. There is the occasional cry of a crow or the gallop of a horse down below, at the foot of the rampart whereon my frail habitation rests, or the passing of an occasional messenger. Otherwise nothing; not a single sound near enough to trouble the sunny quiet of my retreat. No surprise is possible, no visitor.

I have been working for an hour, when a light rustling behind me from the direction of the entrance gives me the feeling of some discreet and agreeable presence. I turn round, and there is a cat who has stopped short with one foot in the air, hesitating and looking me straight in the eye, as if to ask: "Who are you, and what are you doing here?"

I call him quietly, he replies with a plaintive miaul; and I, always tactful with cats, go on with my writing, knowing very well that in a first interview one must not be too insistent.

He is a very pretty cat, yellow and white, with the distinguished and elegant air of a grand seignior. A moment later and he is rubbing against my leg; so then I put my hand slowly down on the small, velvety head, which, after a sudden start, permits my caresses and abandons itself to them. It is over; the acquaintance is made. He is evidently a cat accustomed to petting, probably an intimate of the Empress. To-morrow and every day I shall beg my orderly to bring him a cold luncheon from my rations.

The illusion of summer ends with the day. The sun sets big and red behind the Lake of the Lotus, all at once taking on a sad, wintry look; at the same time a chill comes over all things, and the empty palace grows suddenly gloomy. For the first time that day I hear footsteps approaching, resounding in the silence on the pavement of the esplanade. My servants, Osman and Renaud, are coming for me according to instructions; they are the only human beings for whom the gate of the walls below has orders to open.

It is icy cold as we cross the Marble Bridge in the twilight to return to our home, and the moisture is gathering in clouds over the lake, as it does every night.

After supper we go on a man hunt in the dark, through the courts and rooms of the place. On the preceding nights we had observed through the transparent window-panes disturbing little lights which were promptly extinguished if we made any noise. These lights moved up and down the uninhabited galleries, some distance away, like fireflies. To-night's effort brings about the capture of three unknown men who with cutlasses and dark lanterns have climbed over the walls to pilfer in the imperial reserves. There are two Chinese and one European, a soldier of one of the allied nations. Not to make too much ado over it, we content ourselves with putting them out after cudgelling them well and boxing their ears.

V

TUESDAY, October 23.

LAST NIGHT THERE was a still harder frost, which covered the ground in the courtyard with small white crystals. This we discover during our regular morning exploration of the galleries and dependencies of the palace.

The former lodgings of the begging missionaries and the schoolrooms are overflowing with packing boxes containing reserve supplies of silk and tea. There is also a heap of old bronzes, vases, and incense-burners piled up to the height of a man.

But the church itself is the most extraordinary mine, — a regular Ali Baba's cave, quite filled. In addition to antiquities brought from the Violet City, the Empress had put there all the presents she received two years ago for her Jubilee. (And the line of mandarins who on that occasion brought presents to their sovereign was a league long and lasted an entire day.)

In the nave and side aisles the boxes and cases are piled to half the height of the columns. In spite of the confusion, in spite of the hasty pillaging of those who have preceded us, — Chinese, Japanese, German, and Russian soldiers, — a marvellous collection remains. The most enormous of the chests, — those beneath, — protected by their weight and by the mass of things on top of them, have not even been opened. The first to go were the innumerable smaller articles on top, most of them enclosed in glass cases or in yellow silk coverings, such as bunches of artificial flowers in agate, jade, coral, or lapis lazuli, pagodas and blue landscapes made of the feathers of the kingfisher marvellously utilized. Works of Chinese patience which have cost years of toil are now broken in bits by the stroke of a bayonet, while the glass which protected them is crackling under one's feet on the floor.

Imperial robes of heavy silk brocaded with gold dragons lie on the ground among cases of every description. We walk over them, we walk over carved ivories, over pearls and embroideries galore. There are bronzes a thousand years old, from the Empress's collection; there are screens which seem to have been carved and embroidered by supernatural beings, there are antique vases, cloisonné, crackle ware, lacquers. Certain of the boxes underneath, bearing the names of emperors who died a century ago, contain presents sent them from distant provinces, which no one has ever taken the trouble to open. The sacristy of this astonishing cathedral contains in a series of pastboard boxes, all the sumptuous costumes for the actors in the Empress's theatre, with many fashionable headdresses of former times.

This church, so full of pagan riches, has kept its organ intact, although it has been silent for thirty years. My comrade mounts with me to the gallery to try the effect of some hymns of Bach and Handel under these vaultings, while the African chasseurs, up to their knees in ivories, silks, and court costumes, continue their task of clearing things out below.

About ten o'clock this morning I cross over to the opposite side of the Violet City to visit the Palace of Ancestors, which is in charge of our marines. This was the Holy of Holies, the Pantheon of dead emperors, a temple which was never even approached.

It is in a particularly shady spot; in front of the entrance gate are light but ornate triumphal arches of green, red, and gold lacquer, resting on frail supports, and mingling with the sombre branches of the trees. Enormous cedars and cypresses, twisted by age, shelter the marble monsters which crouch at the threshold and have given them a greenish hue.

Passing the first enclosure, we naturally find a second. The courts, always shaded by old trees, succeed one another in solemn magnificence. They are paved with large stones, between which grows a weed common in cemeteries; each one of the cedars and cypresses which cast its shadow here is surrounded by a marble circle and seems to spring from a bed of carving. A thick layer of thousands of pine needles continually falling from the branches, covers everything. Gigantic incense-burners of dull bronze, centuries old, rest on pedestals bearing emblems of death.

Everything here has an unprecedented stamp of antiquity and mystery. It is a unique place, haunted by the ghosts of the Chinese emperors.

On each side are secondary temples, whose walls of lacquer and gold have taken on with time the shades of old Cordova leather. They contain broken catafalques, emblems and objects pertaining to certain funeral rites.

It is all incomprehensible and terrible; one feels profoundly incapable of grasping the meaning of these forms and symbols.

At length, in the last court on a white marble terrace guarded by bronze roes, the Ancestors' Palace lifts its tarnished gold façade, surmounted by a roof of yellow lacquer.

It consists of one immense room, grand and gloomy, all in faded gold turning to coppery red. At the rear is a row of nine mysterious double doors, which are sealed with wax. In the centre are the tables on which the repasts for the ancestral shades were placed, and where, on the day the Yellow City was taken, our hungry soldiers rejoiced to find an unexpected meal set forth. At each extremity of this lofty room chimes and stringed instruments await the hour, which may never come again, when they shall make music for the Shades. There are long, horizontal zithers, grave in tone, which are supported by golden monsters with closed eyes; gigantic chimes, one of bells, the others of marble slabs and jade, suspended by gold chains and surmounted by great fantastic beasts spreading their golden wings toward the dusky gold ceiling.

There are also lacquered cupboards as big as houses, containing collections of old paintings, rolled on ebony or ivory sticks, and wrapped in imperial silks.

Some of these are marvellous, and are a revelation of Chinese art of which we of the Occident have no conception, — an art at least equal to our own, though profoundly unlike it. Portraits of emperors in silent revery, or hunting in the forest, portray wild places which give one a longing for primitive nature, for the unspoiled world of rocks and trees. Portraits of dead empresses painted in water-colors on faded silks recall the candid grace of the Italian Primitives, — portraits so pale, so colorless, as to seem like fleeting reflections of persons, yet showing a perfection of modelling attained with absolute simplicity, and with a look of concentration in the eye that makes you feel the likeness and enables you for one strange moment to live face to face with these princesses of the past who have slept for centuries in this splendid mausoleum. All these paintings were sacred, never seen or even suspected to exist by Europeans.

Other rolls, which when spread out on the pavement are six or eight metres long, represent processions, receptions at court, or lines of ambassadors; cavaliers, armies, banners; men of all kinds by the thousands, whose dress, embroideries, and arms, suggest that one should look at them with a magnifying glass. The whole history of Chinese costume and ceremonial is contained in these precious miniatures. We even find here the reception, by I know not what emperor, of an ambassador from Louis XIV.; small persons with very French faces are represented as though for exhibition at Versailles, with wigs after the fashion of Roi-Soleil.

The nine magnificent sealed doors at the back of the temple, shut off the altars of nine emperors. They were good enough to break the red wax seals for me and to destroy the fastenings at one of the forbidden entrances, so that I might penetrate into one of the sacred sanctuaries, — that of the great Emperor Kouang-Lu, who was in his glory at the beginning of the eighteenth century. A serjeant has orders to accompany me in this profanation, holding in his hand a lighted candle, which seems to burn reluctantly here in the light cold air of the tomb. The temple itself was quite dark, but here it was black night itself, and it seemed as though dirt and cinders had been thrown about; the dust that accumulates so endlessly in Pekin seems a sign of death and decay. Passing from daylight, however dim, to the light of one small candle that is lost in the shadows, one sees confusedly at first, and there is a momentary hesitation, especially if the place is startling in itself. I see before me a staircase rising to a sort of tabernacle, which seems to be full of artistic creations of some unknown kind.

At both right and left, closed by complicated locks, are some severe chests which I am permitted to examine. In their compartments and in their double secret bottoms the sovereign's imperial seals have been concealed by the hundreds, — heavy seals of onyx, jade, or gold struck off for every occasion of his life and in commemoration of all the acts of his reign; priceless relics which no one dared touch after his obsequies, and which have lain there for twice one hundred years.

I go up into the tabernacle and the serjeant holds his candle before the marvels there, — jade sceptres and vases, some of a peculiar and exquisite workmanship in both dark and light jade, in cloisonné on gold, or in plain solid gold. Behind the altar in an obscure position a grand figure which I had not perceived followed me with an oblique look that reached me through two curtains of yellow imperial silk, whose folds were black with dust. It is a pale portrait of the defunct Emperor, — a life-sized portrait, so obscure, as seen by the light of our single wretched candle, as to seem like the reflection of a ghost in a tarnished mirror. What a nameless sacrilege would our opening the chests where his treasures were hidden seem to this dead man, nay, even our presence in this most impenetrable of all places in an impenetrable city!

When everything is carefully closed again, when the red seals have been put back in place and the pale image of the Emperor returned to silence, to its customary shadows, I hasten to get away from the tomblike chill, to breathe the air again, to seek on the terrace some of the autumn sunshine which filters through the cedar branches.

I am going to take breakfast to-day with the French officers at the extreme north end of the imperial wood, at the Temple of the Silkworm. This, too, is an admirable old sanctuary, preceded by sumptuous courts with marble terraces and bronze vases. This Yellow City is a complete world of temples and palaces set in green. Up to last month the travellers who thought they were seeing China, and to whom all this remained closed, forbidden, could have no idea of the marvellous city opened to us by the war.

When I start back to my Palace of the Rotunda, about two o'clock, a burning sun is shining on the dark cedars and willows; one seeks shade as if it were summer, and the willows are losing many of their leaves. At the entrance to the Marble Bridge, not far from my gate, the two bodies in blue gowns which lie among the lotus are bathed in an ironical splendor of light.

After the soldiers on guard have closed the low postern by which one gains access to my high garden, I am again alone in the silence until the sun's rays, falling oblique and red upon my writing-table, announce the coming of the melancholy evening.

I am scarcely seated at my work before a friendly head, discreetly rubbed against my leg to attract my attention, announces the visit of the cat. I am not unprepared for this visit, for I now expect it every day.

An hour of ideal quiet goes by, broken only by two or three ravens' cries. Then I hear the noise of cavalry galloping over the stone pavements at the foot of my wall; it proves to be Field-Marshal von Waldersee, followed by an escort of soldiers with small flags at the tips of their spears. He is returning to the palace where he lives, not far from here, one of the most sumptuous of all the residences of the Empress. My eyes follow the cavalcade as it crosses the Marble Bridge, turns to the left, and is lost behind the trees. Then the silence returns, absolute as before.

From time to time I go out to walk on my high terrace, and always discover there something new. There are enormous tam-tams under my cedars, with which to call upon the gods; there are beds of yellow chrysanthemums and Indian-yellow carnations, upon which the frost has left a few flowers; there is a kind of dais of marble and faience supporting an object quite indefinite at first sight, — one of the largest blocks of jade in the world, cut in imitation of an ocean wave with monsters struggling in the foam.

I visit some deserted kiosks, — still furnished with ebony thrones, divans, and yellow silk cushions, — which seem like little clandestine love nests. There is no doubt that the beautiful sovereign, passionate still, though aging, used to isolate herself here with her favorites among the imperial silks in these protecting shadows.

My only companion in my palace of dreams to-day is the big alabaster goddess robed in gold, who perpetually smiles upon broken vases and withered flowers; her temple, where the sun never enters, is always cold and grows dark before it should.

But now real night has come, and I begin to feel chilly. The sun, which in France is at its meridional apogee, is sinking; sinking here, a big red ball without light or heat, going down behind the Lake of the Lotus in a wintry mist.

The chill of the night comes on suddenly, giving me the sensation of an abrupt descent into a cave of ice and a furtive little feeling of anguish at being exiled so far from home.

I greet my two servants like friends when they come for me, bringing a cape for me to wear on the way back to the palace.

VI

WEDNESDAY, October 24.

THE SAME GLORIOUS sunshine in gallery, garden, and wood. Each day the work of our soldiers with their gangs of Chinese laborers goes on in the nave of the Cathedral; they carefully separate such treasures as have remained intact, or nearly so, from what is irreparably injured. There is a continual coming and going across our court of furniture and precious bronzes in hand-barrows; all that is taken out of the church is put in places not at present needed for our troops, to await its final transportation to the Ancestors' Palace, where it is to remain under lock and key.

We have seen so many of these magnificent things that we are satiated and worn with them. The most remarkable discoveries made from the depths of the oldest cases have ceased to astonish us; there is nothing now that we want for the decoration — oh, so fleeting — of our apartments; nothing is sufficiently beautiful for our Heliogabalean fancies. There will be no to-morrow, for the inventory must be finished within a few days, and then our long galleries will be parcelled out for officers' rooms and offices.

In the way of discoveries, we came this morning upon a pile of bodies, — the last defenders of the Imperial City, who fell all in a heap and have remained in positions indicative of extreme agony. The crows and the dogs have gone down into the ditch where they lie and have devoured eyes, chests, and intestines; there is no flesh left on their bones, and their red spinal columns show through their ragged raiment. Shoes are left, but no hair; Chinamen have evidently descended into the deep hole with the dogs and the crows, and have scalped the dead in order to make false queues.

To-day I leave the Palace of the North early and for all day, as I must go over to the European quarter to see our Minister at the Spanish legation, where he was taken in; he is still in bed, but convalescing so that at last I can make to him the communications which I undertook on behalf of the admiral.

For four days I have not been outside the red walls of the Imperial City, have not left our superb solitude. So when I find myself once more among the ugly gray ruins of the commonplace streets of the Tartar City, in everybody's Pekin, in the Pekin known to all travellers, I appreciate better the unique peculiarities of our great wood, of our lake, and of all our forbidden glories.

However, this city of the people seems less forlorn than on the day of my arrival in the wind and snow. The people are beginning to return, as I have been told; Pekin is being re-populated, the shops are opening, houses are rebuilding, and already a few humble and entertaining trades have been taken up along the streets, on tables, under tents, and under parasols. The warm sunshine of the Chinese autumn is the friend of many a poor wretch who has no fire.

VII

THE TEMPLE OF THE LAMAS

THE TEMPLE OF the Lamas, the oldest sanctuary in Pekin, and one of the most curious in the world, contains a profusion of marvellous work of the old Chinese gold and silver smiths, and a library of inestimable value.

This precious temple has seldom been seen, although it has been in existence for centuries. Before this year's European invasion, access to it was strictly forbidden to "outside barbarians," and even since the Allies have had possession of Pekin, very few have ever gone there. It is protected by its location in an angle of the Tartar wall in quite a lifeless part of the city whose different quarters are dying from century to century as old trees lose their branches one by one.

Going there to-day on a pilgrimage with the members of the French legation, we find that we are all there for the first time.

In order to reach it we first cross the eastern market-place, three or four kilometres through a sunless and desolate Pekin, — a Pekin that bears the marks of war and defeat, and where things are spread out for sale on the filth and ashes of the ground. Some matchless objects transmitted by one generation of mandarins to another are to be found among the rags and old iron; ancient palaces, as well as the houses of the poor, have emptied here some of their most astonishing contents; the sordid and the marvellous lie side by side, — here some pestilential rags, there a bibelot three thousand years old. Along the walls of the houses as far as one can see, the cast-off garments of dead men and women are hung. It is a place for the sale of extravagant clothing without end, opulent furs from Mongolia stolen from the rich, gay costumes of a courtesan, or magnificent heavy silk robes which belonged to great ladies who have disappeared. The Chinese populace, who have done a hundred times more than the invaders in the way of pillage, burning, and destruction in Pekin, the uniformly dirty populace, dressed in blue cotton, with squinting, evil eyes, swarm and crawl about, eagerly searching and raising a perfect cloud of microbes and dust. Ignoble scoundrels with long queues circulate amongst the crowd, offering robes of ermine or blue-fox, or admirable sables for a few piasters, in their eagerness to be rid of stolen goods.

As we approach the object of our journey it grows more quiet; the busy, crowded streets are gradually succeeded by streets that have perished of old age, where there are no passers; grass grows on the thresholds and behind abandoned walls; we see trees with branches knotted like the arms of the aged.

We dismount before a crumbling entrance which seems to open into a park which might be a ghosts' walk; and this is the entrance to the temple.

What sort of a reception shall we have in this mysterious enclosure? We do not know; and at first there is no one to receive us. But the chief of the Lamas soon appears, bowing, with his keys, and we follow him across the funereal park.

With a violet dress, a shaven head, and a face like old wax, at once smiling, frightened, and hostile, he conducts us to a second door, opening into an immense court paved with white stones, completely surrounded by the curious walls of the first buildings of the temple. Their foundations are massive, their roofs curved and forked, the walls themselves awe-inspiring on account of their size, and hermetically sealed; and all this is the color of ochre and rust, with golden reflections thrown on the high roofs by the evening sun.

The court is deserted, the grass grows between the paving-stones. On the white marble balustrades in front of the closed doors of these great temples are ranged "prayer-mills," which are conical thrones made of bronze, and engraved with secret symbols, which the priests turn and turn while murmuring words unintelligible to men of our day.

In old Asia, which is our ancestor, I have penetrated to the heart of ancient sanctuaries, trembling meanwhile with indefinable anguish before symbols whose meaning has been lost for centuries. This kind of anguish has never been so tinged with melancholy as to-night, standing before this row of silent "prayer-mills" in the cold, the wind, the solitude, the dilapidation of this court, with its white grass-grown pavement and mysterious yellow walls.

Young Lamas appear one after the other as noiselessly as shadows, and even Lama children, for they begin to instruct them quite young in the old rites no longer understood by any one.

They are young, but they have no appearance of youth; senility is upon them as well as a look of I know not what of mystical dulness; their gaze seems to have come from past centuries and to have lost its clearness on the way. Whether from poverty or renunciation, the yellow gowns that cover their thin bodies are faded and torn. Their faces and their dress, as well as their religion and their sanctuary, are covered, so to speak, with the ashes of time.

They are glad to show us all that we wish to see in their old buildings; and we begin with the study-rooms, where so many generations of obscure and unprogressive priests have been slowly formed.

By looking closely, it is plain that all these walls, now the color of the oxydized metal, were once covered with beautiful designs in lacquer and gilt; to harmonize them all into the present old-bronze shades has required an indefinite succession of burning summers and glacial winters, together with the dust, — the incessant dust blown across Pekin from the deserts of Mongolia.

Their study-rooms are very dark, — anything else would have surprised us; and this explains why their eyes protrude so from their drooping lids. Very dark these rooms are, but immense; sumptuous still, in spite of their neglect, and conceived on a grand scale, as are all the monuments of this city, which was in its day the most magnificent in the world. The high ceilings are supported by lacquered columns. There are small seats for the students, and carved desks by the hundred, all arranged in rows and worn and defaced by long use. Gods in golden robes are seated in the corners. The wall hangings of priceless old work represent the joys of Nirvana. The libraries are overflowing with old manuscripts, some in the form of books, and others in great rolls wrapped up in colored silks.

We are shown into the first temple, which, as soon as the door is opened, shines with a golden glow, — the glow of gold used discreetly, and with the warm, reddish tones which lacquer takes on in the course of centuries. There are three golden altars, on which are enthroned in the midst of a pleiad of small golden gods three great ones, with downcast eyes. The straight stems of the gold flowers standing in gold vases in front of the altars are of archaic stiffness. The repetition, the persistent multiplication of the same objects, attitudes, and faces, is one of the characteristics of the unchanging art of pagodas. As is the case with all the temples of the past, there is here no opening for the light; only the light that comes in through the half-opened doors illumines from below the smile of the great seated idols, and shows dimly the decorations of the ceiling. Nothing has been touched, nothing taken away, not even the admirable cloisonné vases where sticks of incense are burning, — evidently this place has been ignored.

Behind this temple, behind its dusty dependencies, in which

the tortures of the Buddhist hell are depicted, the Lamas conduct us to a second court, paved in white stones, similar in every way to the first; the same dilapidation, the same solitude, the same coppery-yellow walls.

After this second court comes another temple, identical with the first, so much so that one wonders if one is not the victim of an illusion; the same figures, the same smiles, the same gold bouquets in vases of gold, — a patient and servile reproduction of the same magnificence.

After this second temple there is a third court, and a third temple exactly like the two others. But the sun is now lower, and lights only the extreme tips of the faience roofs and the thousands of small monsters of yellow enamel which seem to be chasing one another over the tiling. The wind increases, and we shiver with cold. The pigeons in the carved cornice begin to seek their nests, and the silent owls wake up and begin to fly about.

As we expected, this last temple — possibly the oldest, certainly the most dilapidated — is only a repetition of the other two, save for an idol in the centre, which, instead of being seated and lifesized, is colossal and standing. The gold ceiling rises from about half the height of the statue into a cupola, also gilded, which forms a sort of box enclosing the upper part of the figure. To see the face one must go close to the altars and look up between the rigid flowers and the incense-burners. It then looks like a Titanic mummy in its case, with a downcast look that makes one nervous. But on looking steadily, it exercises a sort of spell; one is hypnotized and held by that smile so impartially bestowed upon all this entourage of dying splendor, gold, dust, cold, twilight, ruins, silence.

VIII

CONFUCIUS

THERE WAS STILL a half-hour of sunshine after we left the ghostly Lamas, so we went to pay a call on Confucius, who dwells in the same quarter, — the same necropolis, one might say, — in an abandonment equally depressing.

The big worm-eaten door slips off its hinges and falls down as we attempt to enter, and an owl who was asleep there takes fright and flies away. Behold us in a sort of mortuary wood, walking over the brown autumn grass.

A triumphal arch is the first thing we come across, built to pay homage to some great Chinese thinker. It is of a charming design, although very peculiar, with three little bell-towers of yellow enamel, which crown the whole, their curved roofs decorated with monsters at each one of the corners.

It stands there like some precious bibelot lost among the ruins. Its freshness is surprising where all else is so dilapidated. One realizes its great age from the archaic nature of its details; but it is made of such enduring materials that the wear and tear of centuries in this dry climate has not affected it. The base is white marble, the rest is of faience, — faience both yellow and green, with lotus leaves, clouds, and chimæras in bold relief.

Farther on is a large rotunda which gives evidence of extreme antiquity; this appears to be the color of dirt or ashes, and is surrounded by a moat where the lotus and the reeds are dying. This is a retreat where wise men may come to meditate upon the vanities of life; the object of the moat is to isolate it and make it more quiet.

It is reached by an arched bridge of marble, with railings that vaguely suggest a succession of animals' heads. Inside, it is deserted, abandoned, crumbling away, and the gold ceiling is full of birds' nests. A really magnificent desk is left, with an arm-chair and a table. It seems as though a kind of fine clay had been scattered by handfuls over everything; the ground is covered with it too, so that one's feet sink into it and one's steps are muffled. We soon discover that there is still a carpet underneath, and that it is really nothing but dust which has been accumulating for centuries, — the thick and ever-present dust which the Mongolian winds blow across Pekin.

After a short walk under the old trees we reach the temple itself, which is preceded by a court surrounded by tall marble pillars. This looks exactly like a cemetery, and yet there are no dead lying under these stele, which are there merely to glorify the memory of the departed. Philosophers who in bygone centuries made this region illustrious by their presence and by their dreams, profound thinkers, lost to us forever, have their names as well as some few of their most transcendent utterances, perpetuated on these stele.

On either side of the white steps leading to the sanctuary, blocks of marble are arranged in the form of a tam-tam. These are so old as to make one's head swim; and upon them maxims intelligible only to a few erudite mandarins have been written in primitive Chinese characters, in letters contemporary with and sisters to the hieroglyphs of Egypt.

This is the temple of disinterestedness, of abstract thought, and of cold speculation. One is struck at once by its absolute simplicity, for which, up to this point, nothing in China has prepared us. Very large, very high as to ceilings, very grand and of a uniform blood-red color, it is magnificently empty and supremely quiet. The columns and walls are red, with a few discreet decorations in gold, dimmed by time and dust. In the centre is a bouquet of gigantic lotus in a colossal vase, and that is all. After the profusion, the debauch of monsters and idols, the multiplication of human and animal forms in the usual Chinese pagoda, this absence of figures of any sort is a comfort and a relief.

In the niches all along the wall there are stele, red like the rest of the place, and consecrated to the memory of persons still more eminent than those of the entrance court, with quotations from their writings carved upon them. The stele of Confucius himself, which is larger than the others, and has longer quotations, occupies the position of honor in the centre of this severe Pantheon, and is placed on a kind of altar.

Properly speaking, this is not a temple; it is not a place for prayer or service. It is rather an academy, a meeting-place for calm, philosophic discussion. In spite of its dust and its abandoned air, it seems that newly elected members of the Academy of Pekin (which is even more than our own the conservator of form and ceremony, I am assured) are still bound to give a conference here.

Besides various maxims of renunciation and wisdom written from top to bottom of the stele, Confucius has left to this sanctuary certain thoughts on literature which have been engraved in letters of gold in such a way as to form pictures hung on the walls.

Here is one which I transcribe for young western scholars who are preoccupied with classification and inquiry. They will find in it a reply twice two thousand years old to one of their favorite questions: "The literature of the future will be the literature of compassion."

It is almost five o'clock when the gloomy, red, autumn sun goes down behind great China on Europe's side, and we leave the temples and the grove behind. I separate from my companions, for they live in the legation quarter in the southern part of the Tartar City, while I go to the Imperial City, far from here.

I have no idea how to get out of this dead region, all new to me, where we have spent the day, and through the lonely labyrinthine streets of Pekin. I have as a guide a "mafou," who has been lent to me, and I only know that I have more than a mile to go before reaching my sumptuous, deserted quarters.

My companions gone, I walk for a few moments in the silent old uninhabited streets before reaching one of the long, broad avenues where blue cotton dresses and long-queued yellow faces begin to appear. There is an interminable row of low houses, wretched, gray things, on either side of the street, where the tramp of horses raises the black friable dust in infectious clouds.

The street is so wide and the houses so low that almost the whole of the twilight sky is visible above our heads; and so suddenly does the cold come on after sunset that in a moment we freeze.

The crowds are dense about the food-shops, and the air is fetid in the neighborhood of the butchers, where dog-meat and roasted grasshoppers are sold. But what good nature in all these people of the streets, who on the day after battle and bombardment permit me to pass without so much as an evil look! What could I do, with my borrowed "mafou" and my revolver, if my appearance did not happen to please them?

For a time after this we are alone in desolate, ruined quarters of the town. According to the position of the pale, setting sun, it seems to me that we are on the right track; but if my "mafou," who speaks nothing but Chinese, has not understood me, I shall be in a predicament.

The return journey in the cold seems interminable to me. At last, however, the artificial mountain of the imperial park is silhouetted in gray on the sky ahead of us, with the little faience kiosks and the twisted trees grouping themselves like scenes painted on lacquer. We reach one of the yellow enamelled gates of the blood-red wall surrounding the Imperial City, where two sentinels of the allied armies present arms. From here I know my way, I am at home; so I dismiss my guide and proceed alone to the Yellow City, from which at this hour no one is allowed to depart.

The Imperial, the Yellow, the Forbidden City, encircled by its own terrible walls in the very heart of great Pekin, with its Babylonian environment, is a park rather than a city, a wood of venerable trees, — sombre cypresses and cedars, — several leagues in circumference. Some ancient temples peep through the branches, and several modern palaces built according to the fancies of the Empress regent. This great forest, to which I return to-night as if it were my home, has at no former period of history been known to foreigners; even ambassadors have never passed its gates; until recently it has been absolutely inaccessible and profoundly unknown to Europeans.

This Yellow City surrounds and protects with its tranquil shadows the still more mysterious Violet City, the residence of the Son of Heaven, which occupies a commanding square in the centre of it, protected by moats and double ramparts.

What silence reigns here at this hour! What a lugubrious region it is! Death hovers over these paths where formerly princesses passed in their palanquins and empresses with their silk-robed followers. Now that the usual inhabitants have fled and Occidental barbarians have taken their places, one meets no one in the woods, unless it be an occasional patrol or a few soldiers of one nation or another, and only the sentinels' step is heard before palace or temple, or the cries of the crows and the barking of dogs about the dead.

I have to cross a region filled with trees, nothing but trees, — trees of a truly Chinese contour, whose aspect is in itself quite sufficient to give one the sharp realization of exile; the road goes on under the deep shadow of the branches that turn the twilight into night. Belated magpies are hopping about on the withered

grass, and the crows, too, their croakings exaggerated by the cold and the silence. At the end of a quarter of an hour a corner of the Violet City appears, just at a turn of the road. She slowly reveals herself, silent, closed, like a colossal tomb. Her long, straight walls are lost in the confusion and obscurity of the distance. As I draw nearer to her the silence seems to be intensified, as though it grew as she broods over it.

One corner of the Lake of the Lotus begins to come out like a bit of mirror placed among the reeds to receive the last reflections of the sky. I must pass along its edges in front of the Island of Jade, which is approached by a marble bridge; and I know in advance, because I have seen it daily, the horrible grimace in store for me from the two monsters who have guarded the bridge for centuries.

At length I emerge from the shadow and oppression of the trees into open space with the clear sky overhead, leaving the lake behind me. The first stars are appearing, indicating another of the nights that pass here in an excess of solitude and silence, with only an occasional gunshot to break the tragic calm of wood and palace.

The Lake of the Lotus, which during the season of flowers must be the marvellous field of pink blossoms described by the poets of China, is now, at the end of October, only a melancholy swamp covered with brown leaves, from which at this hour a wintry mist rises that hangs like a cloud over the dead reeds.

My dwelling is on the other side of the lake; and now I have reached the Marble Bridge which spans it with a beautiful curve, — a curve that stands out white in spite of the darkness.

At this point a corpse-like smell greets my nostrils. For a week I have known whence it comes, — from a person in a blue gown lying with outspread arms, face downward, on the slimy shore; and ten steps farther on his comrade is lying in the grass.

As soon as I cross the beautiful lonely Marble Bridge through the pale cloud that hangs over the water I shall be almost home. At my left is a faience gateway guarded by two German sentinels, — two living beings whom I shall not be sorry to see, — who will salute me in automatic unison; this will be at the entrance to the garden where Field-Marshal von Waldersee resides, in one of the Empress's palaces.

Two hundred metres farther on, after passing more gates and more ruins, I shall come to a fresh opening in an old wall, which will be my entrance, guarded by one of our own men, — an African chasseur. Another of the Empress's palaces is there concealed by its surroundings, — a frail palace, almost wholly enclosed in glass. Once there, I push open a glass door decorated with pink lotus flowers, and find again my nightly fairyland, where priceless porcelains, cloisonné, and lacquer stand about in profusion on the yellow carpets under the wonderfully carved arches of ebony.

<h2 style="text-align:center">IX</h2>

IT IS DARK when I reach my dwelling-place. The fires are already lighted in the subterranean furnaces, and a soft heat rises through the thick yellow carpets. We feel much at home and quite comfortable now in this palace, which at first seemed so dreary to us.

I dine, as usual, at a small ebony table, which is lost in the long gallery so dark at either end, in company with my comrade, Captain C., who has discovered new and wonderful treasures during the day, which he has spread out, that we may enjoy them for at least an evening.

First, there is a throne of a style unknown to us; some screens of colossal size that rest in ebony sockets, on which shining birds are battling with monkeys amid the flowers of a dream. Candelabra, which have remained in their silk cases since the seventeenth century, now hang from the arches above our heads, — a shower of pearls and enamel, — and many other indescribable things added to-day to our wealth of articles of antique art.

It is the last time we shall be able to enjoy our gallery in its completeness, for to-morrow most of these objects are to be labelled and sent off with the reserve stock. Retaining one salon for the general, who is to winter here, the rest of this wing of the palace is to be cut up by light partitions into lodgings and offices for the staff. This work will be done under the direction of Captain C., who is chief architect and supervisor, whilst I, a passing guest, will have only a consulting voice.

As this evening marks the last chapter of our imperial phantasmagoria, we sit up later than usual. For this once we are childish enough to array ourselves in sumptuous Asiatic garments, then we throw ourselves down on the cushions and call opium — so favorable to weary and blasé imaginations such as ours have unfortunately begun to be — to our aid. Alas! to be alone in this palace would have seemed magical enough to us a few years ago without the aid of any avatar.

The opium, needless to say, is of exquisite quality; its fumes, rising in rapid little spirals, soon make the air sweet and heavy. It quickly brings to us the ecstasy, the forgetfulness, the relief, the youthful lightness so dear to the Chinese.

There is absolute silence without; absolute silence and deserted courts, where all is cold and black. The gallery grows warm, the heat of the furnace is heavy, for these walls of glass and paper, so frail as a protection against surprises from without, form rooms almost hermetically sealed and propitious to the intoxication that comes from perfumes.

Stretched out upon the silken cushions, we gaze at the receding ceiling, at the row of arches so elaborately carved into lacework, from which the lanterns with the dangling pearls are suspended. Chimæras of gold stand out from the thick folds of the green or yellow silks. High screens of cloisonné, lacquer, or ebony, the great luxury of China, shut off the corners, forming luxurious nooks filled with jars, bronzes, and monsters with eyes of jade, — eyes which squintingly follow you.

Absolute silence, except that from a distance one of those shots is heard which never fails to mark the torpor of the night, or a cry of distress or alarm; skirmishes between Europeans in the posts and thieving Chinamen; sentinels afraid of the dead or of the night shooting at a shadow.

In the foreground, which is lighted by one lamp, the only luminous things whose design and color are engraved upon our already fixed gaze are four gigantic incense-burners — hieratic in form, and made of an adorable blue cloisonné — resting on gold elephants. They stand out against a background of black lacquer traversed by flying birds, whose plumage is made of different kinds of mother-of-pearl. No doubt our lamp is going out, for, with the exception of these nearer things, we scarcely see the magnificence of the place until the outline of some rare vase five hundred years old, the reflection of a piece of inimitable silk, or the brilliancy of some bit of enamel recalls it to our memory.

The fumes of the opium keep us awake until very late, in a state of mind that is both lucid and at the same time confused. We have never until now understood Chinese art; it is revealed to us for the first time to-night. In the beginning we were ignorant, as is all the world, of its almost terrible grandeur until we saw the Imperial City and the walled palace of the Son of Heaven; now at this nocturnal hour, amid the fragrant fumes that rise in clouds in our over-heated gallery, our impressions of the big sombre temples, of the yellow enamelled roofs crowning the Titanic buildings that rise above terraces of marble, are exalted above mere captivated admiration to respect and awe.

In the thousand details of its embroidery and carvings which surround us in such profusion, we learn how skilful and how exact this art is in rendering the grace of flowers, exaggerating their superb and languishing poses and their deep or deliciously pale colorings; then in order to make clear the cruelty of every kind of living thing, down to dragons and butterflies, they place claws, horns, terrible smiles, and leering eyes upon them! They are right; these embroideries on our cushions *are* roses, lotus flowers, chrysanthemums! As for the insects, the scarabs, the flies, and the moths, they are just like those horrid things painted in gold relief on our court fans.

When we arrive at that special form of physical prostration which sets the mind free (disengages the astral body, they say at Benares), everything in the palace, as well as in the outside world, seems easy and amusing. We congratulate ourselves upon having come to live in the Yellow City at so unique a period in the history of China, at a moment when everything is free, and we are left almost alone to gratify our whims and curiosity. Life seems to hold to-morrows filled with new and interesting circumstances. In our conversation we find words, formulas, images, to express the inexpressible, the things that have never been said. The hopelessness, the misery that one carries about like the weight on a convict's leg, is incontestably lessened; and as to the small annoyances of the moment, the little pin-pricks, they exist no longer. For example, when we see through the glass gallery the pale light of a moving lantern in a distant part of our palace, we say without the slightest feeling of disturbance: "More thieves! They must see us. We'll hunt them down to-morrow!"

And it seems of no consequence, even comfortable to us, that our cushions and our imperial silks are shut off from the cold and the horrors by nothing but panes of glass.

III

X

THURSDAY, October 25.

I HAVE WORKED all day, with only my cat for company, in the solitude of the Rotunda Palace that I deserted yesterday.

At the hour when the red sun is setting behind the Lake of the Lotus my two servants come as usual to get me. But this time, after crossing the Marble Bridge, we pass the turn which leads to my palace, for I have to pay a visit to Monsignor Favier, the Bishop of Pekin, who lives in our vicinity, outside yet quite near the Imperial City.

It is twilight by the time we reach the "Catholic Concession," where the missionaries and their little band of yellow followers endured the stress of a long siege. The cathedral, riddled with balls, has a vague look against the dark sky; and it is so dusty that we see as through a fog this newly built cathedral, the one the Empress paid for in place of the one she took for a storehouse.

Monsignor Favier, the head of the French missions, has lived in Pekin for forty years, has enjoyed for a long time the favor of the sovereigns, and was the first to foresee and denounce the Boxer peril. In spite of the temporary blow to his work, he is still a power in China, where the title of Viceroy was at one time conferred upon him.

The white-walled room where he receives me, lately pierced by a cannon-ball, contains some precious Chinese bibelots, whose presence here astonishes every one at first. He collected them in other days, and is selling them now in order to be able to assist several thousand hungry people driven by the war into his church.

The bishop is a tall man, with fine, regular features, and eyes that show shrewdness and energy. He must resemble in looks, as well as in his determined will, those bishops of the Middle

Ages who went on Crusades to the Holy Land. It is only since the outbreak of hostilities against the Christians that he has resumed the priests' cloth and cut off his long Chinese queue. Permission to wear the queue and the Mandarins' garb was one of the greatest and most subversive favors accorded the Lazarists by the Celestial emperors.

He was good enough to keep me with him for an hour. A well-dressed Chinese served us with tea while he told me of the recent tragedy; of the defence of fourteen hundred metres of wall, organized out of nothing by a young ensign and thirty sailors, of their holding out for two or three months right in the heart of an enflamed city, against thousands of enemies wild with fury. Although he tells it all in a very low tone, his speech grows warmer, and vibrates with a sort of soldierly ruggedness as some emotion chokes him, especially whenever he mentions Ensign Henry.

Ensign Henry died, pierced by two balls, at the end of the last great fight. Of his thirty sailors many were killed, and almost all were wounded. This story of a summer should be written somewhere in letters of gold, lest it should be too quickly forgotten; it should be attested, lest some day it should no longer be believed.

The sailors under the command of this young officer were not picked men; they were the first that came, selected hap-hazard on board ship. A few noble priests shared their vigils, a few brave seminarists took a turn under their orders, besides a horde of Chinese armed with miserable old guns. But the sailors were the heart and soul of this obstinate defence; there was neither weakening nor complaint in the face of death, which was at all times present in its most atrocious forms.

An officer and ten Italian soldiers brought hither by chance also fought heroically, leaving six of their number among the dead.

Oh, the heroism, the lowly heroism of these poor Chinese Christians, both Catholic and Protestant, who sought protection in the bishop's palace, knowing that one word of abjuration, one reverence to a Buddhist image would ensure their lives, yet who remained there, faithful, in spite of gnawing hunger and almost certain martyrdom! And at the same time, outside of these walls which protected them in a measure, fifteen thousand of their brothers were burned, dismembered, and thrown piecemeal into the river on account of the new faith which they would not renounce.

Unheard-of things happened during this siege: a bishop[1],followed by an ensign and four marines, went to wrest a cannon from the enemy, balls grazing their heads; theological students manufactured powder from the charred branches of the trees in the close, and from saltpetre, which they scaled the walls to steal at night from a Chinese arsenal.

They lived in a continual tumult under a continual fire of stones and shot; all the marble belltowers of the cathedral, riddled by shells, tottered and fell piecemeal upon their heads. At all hours, without truce, bullets rained in the court, breaking in the roofs and weakening the walls. At night especially balls fell like hailstones to the sound of the Boxers' trumpets and frightful gongs. And all the while their death-cries, "Cha! Cha!" (Let us kill, let us kill) or "Chao! Chao!" (Let us burn, let us burn) filled the city like the cries of an enormous pack of hounds.

It was in July and August under a burning sky, and they lived surrounded by fire; incendiaries sprinkled their roofs and their entrances with petroleum by means of pumps and threw lighted torches onto them; they were obliged to run from one place to another and to climb up with ladders and wet blankets to put

---

1 Monsignor Jarlin, the coadjutor of Monsignor Favier.

out the flames. They had to run, run all the time, when they were so exhausted and their heads so heavy from having had no food, that they could scarcely stand.

Even the good Sisters had to organize a kind of race for the women and children, who were stupefied from fear and suffering. It was these sublime women who decided when it was necessary to change positions according to the direction from which the shells came and who chose the least dangerous moment to fly, with bowed heads, across a court, and to take refuge elsewhere. A thousand women without wills or ideas of their own, with poor dying babies clinging to their breasts, followed them; a human eddy, advancing, receding, pushing, in order to keep in sight the white caps of their protectors.

They had to run when, from lack of food, they could scarcely stand, and when a supreme lassitude impelled them to lie down on the ground to await death! They had to become accustomed to detonations that never ceased, to perpetual noise, to shot and shell, to the fall of stones, to seeing one of their number fall bathed in his own blood! Hunger was the most intolerable of all. They made soup of the leaves and young branches of the trees, of dahlia roots from the gardens and of lily bulbs. The poor Chinese would say humbly, "We must keep the little grain we have left for the sailors who are protecting us, and whose need of strength is greater than ours."

The bishop told of a poor woman who had been confined the previous night, who dragged herself after him imploring: "Bishop, bishop, give me a handful of grain so that my milk will come and my child may not die!"

All night long the feeble voices of several hundred children were heard in the church moaning for lack of food. To use the expression of Monsignor Favier, it was like "the bleatings of a flock of lambs about to be sacrificed." But their cries diminished, for they were buried at the rate of fifteen in a single day.

They knew that not far away in the European legations a similar drama was being enacted, but, needless to say, there was no communication between them; and if any young Chinese Christian offered to go there with a message from the bishop asking for help, or at least for news, it was not long before they saw his head, with the note pinned to his cheek, reappear above the wall at the end of a rod garnished with his entrails.

Not only did bullets rain by the hundreds every day, but the Boxers put anything that fell into their furious hands into their cannon, — stones, bricks, bits of iron, old kettles. The besieged had no doctors; they hopelessly, and as best they could, bound up great horrible wounds, great holes in the breast. The arms of the voluntary gravediggers were exhausted with digging places in which to bury the dead, or parts of the dead. And the cry of the infuriated mob went on, "Cha! Cha!" (Let us kill, let us kill!) to the grim sounds of their iron gongs and the blasts of their trumpets.

Mines went off in different localities, swallowing up people and bits of wall. In the gulf made by one of them fifty little babies in their cradles disappeared. Their sufferings at least were over. Each time a new breach was made the Boxers threw themselves upon it, and it became a yawning opportunity for torture and death.

But Ensign Henry was always there; with such of his sailors as had been spared he was seen rushing to the place where he was needed, to the exact spot where the most effective work could be done, — on a roof or on the crest of a wall, — and they killed and they killed, without losing a ball, every shot dealing death. Fifty, a hundred of them, crouched in heaps on the ground; priests and Chinese women, as well as men, brought stones, bricks, marble, no matter what, from the cathedral, and with the mortar they had ready they closed the breach and were saved again until the next mine exploded!

But they came to the end of their strength, the meagre ration of soup grew less and less, and they could do no more.

The bodies of Boxers, piled up along the vast enclosure which they so desperately defended, filled the air with a pestilential odor; dogs were attracted and gathered in moments of calm for a meal. During the latter part of the time they killed these dogs from the tops of the walls and pulled them in by means of a hook at the end of a cord, and their meat was saved for the sick and for nursing mothers.

On the day when our soldiers at last entered the place, guided by the white-haired bishop standing on the wall and waving the French flag, on the day when they threw themselves with tears of joy in one another's arms, there remained just enough food to make, with the addition of many leaves, one last meal.

"It seemed," said Monsignor Favier, "as though Providence had counted the grains of rice."

Then he spoke once more of Ensign Henry. "The only time during the entire siege," he said, "the only time we wept was when he died. He remained on his feet giving his orders, although mortally wounded in two places. When the fight was over he came down from the breach and fell exhausted in the arms of two of the priests; then we all wept with the sailors, who had come up and surrounded him. He was so charming, simple, good, and gentle with even the humblest. To be a soldier such as he was, to make yourself loved like a little child, could there be anything more beautiful?" Then after a silence he added, "And he had faith; every morning he used to come with us to prayers and to communion, saying with a smile, 'One must be always ready.' "

It is quite dark before I take leave of the bishop, on whom I had intended to pay a short call. All around him now, of course, everything is desolate and in ruins; there are no houses left, and the streets cannot even be traced. I go away with my two servants, our revolvers and one little lantern; I go thinking of Ensign Henry, of his glory, of his deliverance, of everything rather than the insignificant detail of the road to be followed among the ruins. Besides, it is not far, scarcely a kilometre.

A violent wind extinguishes the candle in its paper sheath, and envelops us in dust so thick that we cannot see two steps in front of us; it is like a thick fog. So, never having been in this quarter before, we are lost, and go stumbling along over stones, over rubbish, over broken pottery, and human bones.

We can scarcely see the stars for the thick cloud of dust, and we don't know which way to go.

Suddenly we get the smell of a dead body and we recognize the ditch we discovered yesterday morning just in time to keep from falling into it. So all is well; only two hundred metres more and we shall be at home in our glass palace.

XI

FRIDAY, October 26.

Leaving my palace a little late, I hasten to keep the appointment made for me by Li-Hung-Chang for nine o'clock in the morning.

An African chasseur accompanies me. Following a Chinese outrider sent to guide us, we start off at a rapid trot through the dust and silence under the sun's white rays, along the great walls and marshy moats of the Emperor's Palace.

When we get outside of the Yellow City noise and life begin again. After the magnificent solitude to which we have become accustomed, whenever we return to everybody's Pekin, we are surprised to find such a roar among these humble crowds; it is hard to realize that the woods, the lakes, the horizons, which play at being the real country, are artificial things surrounded on all sides by the most swarming of cities.

It is incontestable that the people are returning in crowds to Pekin. (According to Monsignor Favier, the Boxers in particular are returning in all kinds of costumes and disguises.) From day to day the number of silk gowns, blue cotton gowns, slanting eyes, and queues increases.

We must move faster in spite of all the people, for it seems it is still some distance, and time is passing. Our outrider appears to be galloping. We cannot see him, for here the streets are even dustier than in the Yellow City; we see only the cloud of dust that envelops his little Mongolian horse, and we follow that.

At the end of half an hour's rapid riding the dust cloud stops in front of a ramshackle old house in a narrow street that leads nowhere. Is it possible that Li-Hung-Chang, rich as Aladdin, the owner of palaces and countless treasures, one of the most enduring favorites of the Empress and one of the glories of China, lives here?

For reasons unknown to me, the entrance is guarded by Cossack soldiers in poor uniforms but with naïve rosy faces. The room into which I am taken is dilapidated and untidy; there is a table in the middle of it and two or three rather well-carved ebony chairs; but that is all. At one end is a chaos of trunks, bags, packages, and bedding, all tied up as though in preparation for flight. The Chinese who comes to the door, in a beautiful gown of plum-colored silk, gives me a seat and offers me tea. He is the interpreter, and speaks French correctly, even elegantly. He tells me that some one has gone to announce me to his Highness.

At a sign from another Chinese he presently conducts me into a second court, and there, at the door leading into a reception-room, a tall old man advances to meet me. At his right and his left are silk-robed servants, both a whole head shorter than he is, on whose shoulders he leans. He is colossal, with very prominent cheek-bones, and small, very small, quick and searching eyes. He is an exaggeration of the Mongolian type, with a certain beauty withal, and the air of a great personage, although his furry gown of an indefinite color is worn and spotted. (I have been forewarned that in these days of abomination his Highness believes that he should affect poverty.) The large shabby room where he receives me is, like the first one, strewn with trunks and packages. We take arm-chairs opposite each other, while servants place cigarettes, tea, and champagne on a table between us. At first we stare at each other like two beings from different worlds.

After inquiring as to my age and the amount of my income (one of the rules of Chinese politeness), he bows again, and conversation begins.

When we have finished discussing the burning questions of the day, Li-Hung-Chang expresses sympathy for China and for ruined Pekin. "Having visited the whole of Europe," he says, "I have seen the museums of all your great capitals. Pekin had her own also, for the whole Yellow City was a museum begun centuries ago, and may be compared with the most beautiful of your own. And now it is destroyed."

He questions me as to what we are doing over in the Palace of the North, informs himself by adroit questioning as to whether we are injuring anything there. He knows as well as I do what we are doing, for he has spies everywhere, even among our workmen; yet his enigmatical face shows some satisfaction when I confirm his knowledge of the fact that we are destroying nothing.

When the audience is over, and we have shaken hands, Li-Hung-Chang, still leaning on his two servants, comes with me as far as the centre of the court. As I turn at the threshold to make my final bow, he courteously recalls to my memory my offer to send him my account of my stay in Pekin, — if ever I find time to write it. In spite of the perfect grace of his reception of me, due especially to my title of "Mandarin of Letters," this old prince of the Chinese Arabian Nights' tales, in his threadbare garments and in his wretched surroundings, has not ceased to seem to me disturbing, inscrutable, and possibly secretly disdainful and ironical, all the time disguising his real self.

I now make my way across two kilometres of rubbish to the quarters of the European legations in order to take leave of the French minister, who is still ill in bed, and to get from him his commissions for the admiral, for I must leave Pekin not later than the day after to-morrow, and go back to my ship.

Just as I was mounting my horse again, after this visit, to return to the Yellow City, some one from the legation came out and very kindly gave me some precise and very curious information which will enable me this evening to purloin two tiny shoes that once belonged to the Empress of China, and to take them away as a part of the pillage. On a shady island in the southern part of the Lake of the Lotus is a frail, almost hidden palace, where the sovereign slept that last agonizing night before her frantic flight, disguised as a beggar. *The second room to the left, at the back of the second court* of this palace, was her room, and there, it seems, under a carved bed, lie two little red silk shoes embroidered with butterflies and flowers, which must have belonged to her.

I return to the Yellow City as fast as I can, breakfast hurriedly in the glass gallery, — whence the wonderful treasures are already being carried to their new quarters to make way for the carpenters, who soon begin their work here, — and straightway depart with my two faithful servants, on foot this time, in search of the island, the palace, and the pair of small shoes.

The one o'clock sun is burning the dry paths, and the cedars

overhead are gray with dust. About two kilometres to the south of our residence we find the island without difficulty. It is in a region where the lake divides into various little arms, spanned by marble bridges with marble railings entwined with green. The palace stands there light and charming, half concealed among the trees, on a terrace of white marble. The roofs of green faience touched with gilt and the open-work walls shine forth with new and costly ornamentation from amid the dusty green of the old cedars. It must have been a marvel of grace and daintiness, and it is adorable as it is, deserted and silent.

Through the doors opening onto the white steps that lead up to it, a perfect cascade of débris of all kinds is tumbling, — boxes of imperial porcelains, boxes of gold lacquer, small bronze dragons upside down, bits of rose-colored silk, and bunches of artificial flowers. Barbarians have been this way, — but which? Surely not our soldiers, for this part of the Yellow City was never placed in their hands; they are not familiar with it.

The interior courts, from which at our approach a flock of crows rise, are in the same condition. The pavement is strewn with delicate, rather feminine things, which have been ruthlessly destroyed. And so recent is this destruction that the light stuffs, the silk flowers, the parts of costumes have not even lost their freshness.

"At the back of the second court, the second room to the left!" Here it is! There remains a throne, some arm-chairs, and a big, low bed, carved by the hand of genius. Everything has been ransacked. The window-glass, through which the sovereign could gaze upon the reflections of the lake and the pink blossoms of the lotus, the marble bridges, the islands, the whole landscape devised and realized for her eyes, has been broken; and a fine white silk, with which the walls were hung, and on which some exquisite artist had painted in pale tints, larger than nature, other lotus blossoms, languishing, bent by the autumn wind, and strewing their petals, has been torn in shreds.

Under the bed, where I look immediately, is a pile of manuscript and charming bits of silk. My two servants, foraging with sticks, like rag-pickers, soon succeed in finding what I seek, — the two comical little red shoes, one after the other.

They are not the absurd, doll-like shoes worn by the Chinese women who compress their toes; the Empress, being a Tartar princess, did not deform her feet, which were, however, very small by nature. No, these are embroidered slippers of natural shape, whose extravagance lies in the heels, which are thirty centimetres high and extend over the entire sole, growing larger at the bottom, like the base of a statue, to prevent the wearer from falling; they are little blocks of white leather of the most improbable description.

I had no idea that a woman's shoes could take up so much space. How to get them away without looking like pillagers in the eyes of the servants and guards we meet on the way back is the question?

Osman suggests suspending them by strings to Renaud's belt so that they will hang concealed by his long winter coat. This is an admirable scheme; he can even walk — we make him try it — without giving rise to suspicion. I feel no remorse, and I fancy that if she, from afar, could witness the scene, the still beautiful Empress would be the first to smile.

We now hasten our steps back to the Palace of the Rotunda, where I have scarcely two hours of daylight for my work before the cold and the night come on.

Each time that I return to this palace I am charmed with the sonorous silence of my high esplanade and with the top of the crenellated wall surrounding it, — an artificial spot whence one commands an extended view of artificial landscape, the sight of which has always been forbidden, and which, until lately, no European has ever seen.

Everything about the place is so Chinese that one feels as though it were the heart of the yellow country, the very quintessence of China. These high gardens were a favorite resort for the ultra-Chinese reveries of an uncompromising Empress who possibly dreamed of shutting her country off from the rest of the world, as in olden times, but who to-day sees her empire crumbling at her feet, rotten to the core, like her myriads of temples and gilded wooden gods.

The magical hour here is when the enormous red ball, which the Chinese sun appears to be on autumn evenings, lights up the roofs of the Violet City before it disappears. I never fail to leave my kiosk at this hour to see once more these effects, unique in all the world.

Compared to this, what barbaric ugliness is offered by a bird's-eye view of one of our European cities, — a mass of ugly gables, tiles, and dirty roofs full of chimneys and stove-pipes, and, as a last horror, electric wires forming a black network! In China, where they are all too scornful of pavements and sewers, everything which rises into the air, into the domain of the ever-watchful and protecting spirits, is always impeccable. And this immense Imperial retreat, empty to-day, now displays for me alone the splendor of its enamelled roofs.

In spite of their age, these pyramids of yellow faience, carved with a grace unknown to us, are still brilliant under the red sun. At each of the corners of the topmost one the ornaments simulate great wings; lower down, toward the outside, are rows of monsters in poses which are copied and recopied, century after century, sacred and unchanging. These pyramids of yellow faience are brilliant. From far off, against the ashy blue sky, clouded by the everlasting dust, it looks like a city of gold; then, as the sun sinks, like a city of copper.

First the silence of it all; then the croakings that begin the moment the ravens go to rest; then the death-like cold that wraps this magnificence of enamel as in a winding-sheet as soon as the sun goes down.

To-night again, when we leave the Rotunda Palace, we pass the Palace of the North without stopping, and go on to Monsignor Favier's.

He receives me in the same white room, where valises and travelling-bags are lying about on the furniture. The bishop leaves to-morrow for Europe, which he has not seen for twelve years. He is going to Rome to see the Pope, and then to France, to raise money for his suffering missions. His great work of over forty years is annihilated, fifteen thousand of his Christian converts massacred; his churches, chapels, hospitals, schools, are all destroyed, razed to the ground; his cemeteries have been violated, and yet, discouraged at nothing, he wishes to begin all over again.

As he conducts me across his garden I admire the beautiful energy with which he says, pointing to the damaged cathedral with its broken cross, which is the only building left standing, gloomily outlined against the evening sky: "I will rebuild, larger and higher, all the churches they have thrown down, and I hope that each movement of violence and hatred against us may carry Christianity one step further on in their country. Possibly they will again destroy my churches; who knows? If so, I will build them up again, and we shall see whether they or I will be the first to weary of it."

He seems very great to me in his determination and in his faith, and I understand that China must reckon with this apostle of the vanguard.

XII

SATURDAY, October 27.

I WANTED TO see the Violet City and its throne rooms once more before going away, and to enter it this time, not by round-about ways and back doors and secret posterns, but by the great avenues and gates that have been for centuries closed, so that I might try to imagine beneath the destruction of to-day what must have been in former times the splendor of the sovereigns' arrival.

No one of our European capitals has been conceived and laid out with such unity and audacity, with the idea of increasing the magnificence of a pageant always dominant, especially that of imparting an imposing effect to the appearance of the Emperor. The throne is here the central idea. This city, as regular as a geometrical figure, seems to have been created solely to enclose and glorify the throne of the Son of Heaven, ruler of four hundred millions of souls; to be its peristyle, to lead up to it by colossal avenues which recall Thebes or Babylon. It is easy to understand why the Chinese ambassadors, who came to visit our kings in the times when their immense country was flourishing, were not particularly dazzled by the sight of the Paris of those days, of the Louvre or of Versailles.

The southern gate of Pekin, by which the processions arrive, lies in the axis of this throne, once so awe-inspiring, and six kilometres of avenues, with gateways and monsters, lead up to it. When one has crossed the wall of the Chinese City by this southern gate, first passing two huge sanctuaries, — the Temple of Agriculture and the Temple of Heaven, — one follows for half an hour the great artery that leads to a second boundary wall, that of the Tartar City, higher and more commanding than the first. An enormous gate looms up, surmounted by a black dungeon, and beyond this the avenue goes on, flawlessly straight and

magnificent, to a third gate in a third wall of a blood-red color, —
the wall of the Imperial City.

Even after entering the Imperial City it is still some distance to
the throne to which one is advancing in a straight line, — to this
throne which dominates everything and which formerly could
never have been seen; but here its presence is indicated by the
surroundings. From this point the number of marble monsters
increases; lions of colossal size grin from their pedestals at right
and at left; there are marble obelisks — monoliths encircled
with dragons — with the same heraldic beast always seated at
the summit, — a thin kind of jackal with long ears, which has
the appearance of barking or howling in the direction of the
extraordinary thing which is on ahead, namely, the throne of
the Emperor. Walls are multiplied, — blood-colored walls thirty
metres thick, — which cross the road, and are surmounted by
queer roofs and pierced by low gates, — narrow ambushes that
send a thrill of terror to your heart. The defending moats at the
foot of the walls have marble bridges, triple like the gates, and
from here on the road is paved with superb big slabs crossing
one another at an angle, like the boards of a parquetry floor.

After it reaches the Imperial City, this avenue, already a
league in length, is absolutely unfrequented, and goes on even
wider than before between long regular buildings intended for
soldiers' barracks. No more little gilded houses, no more small
shops, no more crowds! At this last imprisoning rampart the
life of the people stops, under the oppression of the throne; and
at the very end of this solitary roadway, watched over by the
slender marble beasts surmounting the obelisks, the forbidden
centre of Pekin becomes visible, the retreat of the Son of Heaven.

The last wall which appears ahead of us — that of the Violet
City — is, like the preceding ones, the color of dried blood; there
are numerous watch-towers upon it, whose roofs of dark enamel

curve up at the corners in wicked little points. The triple gates are too small, too low for the height of the wall, too deep and tunnel-like. Oh, the heaviness, the hugeness of it all, and the strangeness of the design of the roofs, so characteristic of the peculiarities of the yellow colossus!

Things must have begun to go to pieces here centuries ago; the red plaster of the walls has fallen in places, or it has become spotted with black; the marble of the obelisks and the great squinting lions could only have grown so yellow under the rains of innumerable seasons, and the green that pushes through wherever the granite is joined, marks with lines of velvet the design of the pavement.

The last triple gates, given over since the defeat to a detachment of American soldiers, will open to-day for any barbarian, such as I, who carries a properly signed permit.

Passing through the tunnels, one enters an immense marble whiteness, — a whiteness that is turning into ivory yellow and is stained by the autumn leaves and the wild growth that has invaded this deserted spot. The place is paved with marble, and straight ahead, rising like a wall, is an extraordinary marble terrace, on which stands the throne room, with its sturdy blood-red columns and its roof of old enamel. This white enclosure is like a cemetery — so much green has pushed its way up between the paving-stones, — where the silence is broken only by the magpies and the crows.

On the ground are ranged blocks of bronze all similar and cone-like in shape; they are simply placed there among the brown leaves and branches, and can be moved about as if they were ninepins. They are used during the formal entry of a procession to mark the line for the flags and the places where even the most magnificent visitors must prostrate themselves when the Son of Heaven deigns to appear, like a god, on top of the marble terrace, surrounded by banners, and in one of those costumes with breastplate of gold, monsters' heads on the shoulders, and gold wings in the headdress, whose superhuman splendor has been transmitted to us by means of the paintings in the Temple of Ancestors.

One mounts to these terraces by staircases of Babylonian proportions and by an "imperial path," reserved for the Emperor alone, that is to say, by an inclined plane made of one block of marble, — one of those untransportable blocks which men in the past possessed the secret of moving. The five-clawed dragon displays his sculptured coils from the top to the bottom of this stone, which cuts the big white staircase into two equal parts, of which it forms the centre, and extends right to the foot of the throne. No Chinese would dare to walk on this "path" by which the emperors descend, pressing the high soles of their shoes on the scales of the heraldic beast, in order not to slip.

The room at the top, open to-day to all the winds that blow and to all the birds of heaven, has, by way of roof, the most prodigious mass of yellow faience that there is in Pekin, and the most bristling with monsters; the ornaments at the corners are shaped like big extended wings. Inside, needless to say, there is that blaze of reddish gold which always pursues one in Chinese palaces. On the ceiling, which is of an intricate design, dragons are everywhere entwined, entangled, interwoven; their claws and their horns appear, mingled with the clouds, and one of them, which is detached from the mass and seems ready to fall, holds in his hanging jaw a gold sphere directly above the throne. The throne, which is of red and gold lacquer, rises in the centre of this shadowy place on a sort of platform; two large screens made of feathers, emblems of sovereignty, stand behind it, and along the steps which lead up to it are incense-burners similar to those placed in pagodas at the feet of the gods.

Like the avenues through which I have come, like the series of bridges and the triple gates, this throne is in the exact centre of Pekin, and represents its soul; were it not for all these walls, all these various enclosures, the Emperor, seated there on this pedestal of lacquer and marble, could see to the farthest extremities of the city, to the farthest openings in the surrounding walls; the tributary sovereigns who come there, the ambassadors, the armies, from the moment of their entrance into Pekin by the southern gate, would be, so to speak, under the inspiration of his invisible eyes.

On the floor a thick carpet of imperial yellow reproduces in a much worn design the battle of the chimæras, the nightmare carved upon the ceiling; it is a carpet made in one piece, an enormous carpet of a wool so thick and close that one's feet sink into it as on a grassy lawn; but it is torn, eaten by moths, with piles of gray dung lying about on it in patches, — for magpies, pigeons, and crows have made their nests in the roof, and on my arrival the place is filled with the whirring of frightened wings up high against the shining beams, amongst the golden dragons and the clouds.

The incomprehensible fact about this palace, to us uninitiated barbarians, is that there are three of these rooms exactly alike, with the same throne, the same carpet, the same ornaments, in the same places; they are preceded by the same great marble courts and are constructed on the same marble terraces; you reach them by the same staircases and by the same imperial paths.

Why should there be three of them? For, of necessity, the first conceals the two others, and in order to pass from the first to the second, or from the second to the third, you must go down each time into a vast gloomy court without any view and then come up again between the piles of ivory-colored marble, so superb, yet so monotonous and oppressive!

There must be some mysterious reason connected with the use of the number three. This repetition produced on our disordered imaginations an effect analogous to that of the three similar sanctuaries and the three similar courts in the great Temple of the Lamas.

I had already seen the private apartments of the young Emperor. Those of the Empress — for she had apartments here too, in addition to the frail palaces her fancy had scattered over the parks of the Yellow City — those of the Empress are less gloomy and much less dark. Room after room exactly alike, with large windows and superb yellow enamelled roofs. Each one has its marble steps, guarded by two lions all shining with gold, and the little gardens which separate them are filled with bronze ornaments, heraldic beasts, phoenixes, or crouching monsters.

Inside are yellow silks and square arm-chairs of the form consecrated by time, unchanging as China itself. On the chests, on the tables, a quantity of precious articles are placed in small glass cases, — because of the perpetual dust of Pekin, — and this makes them as cheerless as mummies and casts over the apartment the chill of a museum. There are many artificial bouquets of chimerical flowers of neutral shades in amber, jade, agate, and moonstones.

The great and inimitable luxury of these palace rooms consists of the series of ebony arches so carved as to seem a bower of dark leaves. In what far-away forest did the trees grow that permitted such groves to be created out of one single piece? And by means of what implements and what patience are they able to carve each stem and each leaf of light bamboo, or each fine needle of the cedar, out of the very heart of the tree, and to add to them birds and butterflies of the most exquisite workmanship?

Behind the sleeping-room of the Empress a kind of dark oratory is filled with Buddhistic divinities on altars. An exquisite

odor still remains, left behind her by the beautiful, passionate, elegant old woman who was queen. Among these gods is a small creature made of very old wood, quite worn and dull from the loss of gilding, who wears about his neck a collar of fine pearls. In front of him is a bunch of dried flowers, — a last offering, one of the guardian eunuchs informs me, made by the Empress to this little old Buddha, who was her favorite fetish, at the supreme moment before her flight from the Violet City.

To-day I have reached this retreat by a very different route from the one I took on my first pilgrimage here, and in going out I must now pass through the quarters where all is walled and rewalled, the gates barricaded and guarded by more and more horrible monsters. Are there hidden princesses and treasures here? There is always the same bloody color on the walls, the same yellow faience on the roofs, and more horns, claws, cruel forms, hyena smiles, projecting teeth, and squinting eyes than ever; the most unimportant things, like bolts and locks, have features that simulate hatred and death.

Everything is perishing from old age; the stones are worn away, the wooden doors are falling into dust. There are some old shadowy courts that are given up to white-bearded octogenarian servants, who have built cabins, where they live like recluses, occupied in training magpies or in cultivating sickly flowers in pots under the eyes of the everlasting grinning old marble and bronze beasts. No cloistered green, no monk's cell, was ever half so gloomy as these little courts, so shut in and so dark, overshadowed for centuries by the uncontrolled caprices of the Chinese emperors. The inexorable sentence, "Leave hope behind, all those who enter here," seems to belong here; as one proceeds, the passages grow narrower and more intricate; it seems as though there were no escape, as though the great locks on the doors would refuse to work, as though the walls would close in upon and crush you.

Yet here I am almost outside, outside the interior wall and through the massive gates that quickly close behind me. Now I am between the second rampart and the first, both equally terrible. I am on the road which makes a circle around this city, — a sort of ominous passageway of great length that runs between two dark red walls and which seems to meet in the distance ahead of me. Human bones and old rags that have been parts of the clothing of soldiers are scattered here and there, and one sees two or three crows and one of the flesh-eating dogs prowling about.

When the boards which barricade the outside gate are let down for me (the gate guarded by the Japanese), I discover, as though on awakening from a dreadful dream, that I am in the park of the Yellow City, in open space under the great cedars.

XIII

SUNDAY, October 28.

THE ISLAND OF Jade, on the Lake of the Lotus, is a rock, artificial perhaps, in spite of its mountainous proportions. Old trees cling to its sides, and old temples loom up toward the sky, while crowning all is a sort of tower or dungeon of colossal size and of a mysterious Baroque design. It may be seen from all points; its excessively Chinese outlines dominate Pekin, and high up on it stands a terrible idol whose threatening attitude and hideous smile look down upon the city. This idol our soldiers call the "big devil of China."

This morning I am climbing up to visit this "big devil."

A bridge of white marble across the reeds and lotus gives access to the Island of Jade. Both ends of the bridge are guarded, needless to say, by marble monsters who leer and squint at any one who has the audacity to pass. The shores of the island rise abruptly underneath the cedar branches, and one begins immediately to climb by means of steps and rock-cut paths. Among the severe trees is a series of marble terraces with bronze incense-burners and occasional pagodas, out of whose obscurity enormous golden idols shine forth.

This Island of Jade, on account of its position of strategic importance, is under military occupation by a company of our marines.

As there is no shelter other than the pagodas, and no camp beds other than the sacred tables, our soldiers have had to put out of doors the entire population of secondary gods in order to make room to lie down on the beautiful red tables at night, and have left only the big, solemn idols on their thrones. So here they are by the hundreds, by the thousands, lined up on the white terraces like playthings. Inside the temples the guns of our men are lying about, and their blankets and their clothing hang on the walls, all around the big idols who have been left in their places. What a heavy smell of leather they have already introduced into these closed sanctuaries, accustomed only to the odor of sandalwood and incense!

Through the twisted branches of the cedars the horizon, which is occasionally visible, is all green, turning to an autumn brown. It is a wood, an infinite wood, out of which here and there roofs of yellow faience emerge. This wood is Pekin; not at all as one imagines it, but Pekin seen from the top of a very sacred place where no Europeans were ever allowed to come.

The rocky soil grows thinner and thinner as one rises toward the "big devil of China," as one approaches the peak of the isolated cone known as the Island of Jade.

This morning I meet, as I climb, a curious band of pilgrims who are coming down; they are Lazarist missionaries in mandarin costume, wearing long queues. With them are several young Chinese Catholic priests who seem frightened at being there; as though, in spite of the Christianity superimposed upon their hereditary beliefs, they were committing some sacrilege by their very presence in so forbidden a spot.

At the foot of the dungeon which crowns these rocks is the kiosk of faience and marble where the "big devil" dwells. It is high up on a narrow terrace in the pure, clear air, from which one overlooks a mass of trees scarcely veiled to-day by the usual mist of dust and sun.

I enter the kiosk where the "big devil" stands, the sole guest of this aerial region. Oh, horrible creature that he is! He is of superhuman size, cast in bronze. Like Shiva, god of death, he dances on dead bodies; he has five or six atrocious faces whose multiplied grins are almost intolerable; he wears a collar of skulls, and is gesticulating with forty arms that hold instruments of torture or heads severed from their bodies.

Such is the protecting divinity chosen by the Chinese to watch over this city, and placed high above all their pyramidal faience roofs, high above all their pagodas and towers, as we in times of faith would have placed the Christ or the Blessed Virgin. It is a tangible symbol of their profound cruelty, the index of the inexplicable cleft in the brain of these people ordinarily so tractable and gentle, so open to the charm of little children and of flowers, but who are capable all at once of gleefully becoming executioners and torturers of the most horrible description.

At my feet Pekin seems like a wood! I had been told of this incomprehensible effect, but my expectations are surpassed. Outside of the parks in the Imperial City, it has not seemed to me that there were many trees around the houses, that is, in the gardens and in the streets. But from here all is submerged in green. Even beyond the walls whose black outlines may be seen in the distance there are more woods, — endless woods.

Toward the east alone lies the gray desert which I came through that snowy morning, and toward the north rise the Mongolian mountains, charming, translucent, and purple against the pale blue sky.

The great straight arteries of the city, drawn according to a singular plan, with a regularity and an amplitude to be found in none of the European capitals, resemble, from the point where I stand, the avenues in a forest, — avenues bordered by various complicated, delicate little fretwork houses of gray pasteboard or of gilt paper. Many of these arteries are dead; in those which are still living, this fact is indicated from my point of view by the constant moving of little brown animals along the earth, recalling the migration of ants; these caravans, which move slowly and quietly away, are scattered to the four corners of China.

A feeling that is akin to regret is mingled with my afternoon's work in the solitude of my lofty palace, — regret for what is about to end, for I am now on the eve of departure. And it will be an end without any possible beginning again, for if I should return to Pekin this palace would be closed to me, or, in any case, I should never again find here such charming solitude.

Yet this distant, inaccessible spot, of which it once would have seemed madness to say that I should ever make it my dwelling-place, has already become very familiar to me, as well as all that belongs here and all that has happened here, — the presence of the great alabaster goddess in the dark temple, the daily visit of the cat, the silence of the surroundings, the mournful light of the October sun, the agonies of the last butterflies as they beat against my window-panes, the manœuvres of the sparrows whose nests are in the enamelled roofs, the blowing of the dead leaves, and the fall of the little balsam needles on the pavement of the esplanade whenever the wind blows. What a strange destiny, when you think of it, has made me master here for a few days!

The splendors of our long gallery in the Palace of the North are a thing of the past. It is already divided by light wooden partitions which may be removed without difficulty if ever the Empress thinks of returning, but which, for the time being, cut it up into rooms and offices. There are still a few magnificent bibelots in the part which is to be the general's salon, but elsewhere it has all been simplified; the silks, the pottery, the screens, the bronzes, duly catalogued, have been removed to a storehouse. Our soldiers have even found European seats among the palace reserves, which they have taken to the future apartments of the staff to make them more habitable. They consist of sofas and arm-chairs, vaguely Henry II. in style, covered with old-gold plush that reminds one of a provincial hotel.

I expect to leave to-morrow morning. When the dinner hour unites us once again, Captain C. and I, seated at our little ebony table, both feel a touch of melancholy at seeing how things have changed about us, and how quickly our dream of being Chinese sovereigns is over.

MONDAY, October 29.

I have postponed my departure for twenty-four hours in order to meet General Vayron, who returns to Pekin this evening, and undertake his commissions for the admiral. So I have an unexpected half-day to spend in my high mirador, and hope for a last visit from my cat, who will find me no more in my accustomed place, neither to-morrow nor ever again. It is now growing colder each day, so that in any case my work-room would not be possible much longer.

Before the doors of this palace close behind me forever I want to take a last walk into all the windings of the terraces, into all the kiosks, so dainty and so charming, in which the Empress no doubt concealed her reveries and her amours.

As I go to take leave of the great white goddess, — the sun already setting, and the roofs of the Violet City bathed in the red golds of evening, — I find the aspect of things about here changed; the soldiers who were on guard at the gate have climbed to the top and are putting her house in order; they have carried off the thousand and one boxes of porcelains and girandoles, the broken vases and the bouquets, and have carefully swept the place. The alabaster goddess, deliciously pale in her golden robes, still smiles, more than ever solitary in her empty temple.

The sun of this last day sets in little wintry clouds that are cold to look at, and the Mongolian wind makes me shiver in my thick cloak as I cross the Marble Bridge on my return to the Palace of the North, where the general with his escort of cavalry has just arrived.

TUESDAY, October 30.

On horseback, at seven in the morning, a changelessly beautiful sun and an icy wind. I start off with my two servants, young Toum, and a small escort of two African chasseurs, who will accompany me as far as my junk. We have about six kilometres to cover before reaching the dreary country. We first cross the Marble Bridge, then, leaving the great Imperial wood, pass through ruined, squalid Pekin in a cloud of dust.

At length, after going through the deep gates in the high outer ramparts, we reach the outside desert, swept by a terrible wind; and here the enormous Mongolian camels, with lions' manes, perpetually file past in a procession, making our horses start with fear.

We reach Tong-Tchow in the afternoon, and silently cross it, ruined and dead, until we come to the banks of the Pei-Ho. There I find my junk under the care of a soldier, — the same junk that brought me from Tien-Tsin with all the necessities for our life on the water intact. Nothing has been taken during my absence but my stock of pure water, — a serious loss for us, but a pardonable theft at a time like this, when the river water is full of danger for our soldiers. As for us, we can drink hot tea.

We call at the office of the commissary to get our rations and to have our papers signed; then we pull up our anchor from the infected bank that breathes of pestilence and death, and begin to float down the river toward the sea.

Although it is colder than it was coming up, it is almost amusing to take up a nomadic life again in our little sarcophagus with its matting roof, and to plunge once more, as night falls, into the immense green solitude of the dark banks as we glide along between them.

WEDNESDAY, October 31.

The morning sun shines on the bridge of a junk that is covered with a thin coating of ice. The thermometer marks 8° above zero, and the wind blows, cruel and violent, but health-giving, we feel sure.

We have the swift current with us, so that the desolate shores, with their ruins and their dead, slip by much more rapidly than on our other journey. We walk on the tow-path from morning until night in order to keep warm, almost abreast of the Chinese who are pulling the rope. There is a fulness of physical life in the wind; one feels light and full of energy.

THURSDAY, November 1.

Our boat trip lasts only forty-eight hours this time, and we have but two frosty nights to sleep under a matting roof through which the shining stars are visible, for toward the end of the second day we enter Tien-Tsin.

Tien-Tsin, where we have to find a shelter for the night, is horribly repopulated since our last stay here. It takes us almost two hours to row across the immense city, working our way amongst myriads of canoes and junks. Both banks are crowded with Chinese, howling, gesticulating, buying, and selling, in spite of the fact that few of the walls or roofs of the houses are left intact.

FRIDAY, November 2.

In spite of the cold wind and the dust, which continues to blow pitilessly, we arrive at Taku, — horrible city, — at the mouth of the river, by midday. But alas! it will be impossible to join the squadron to-day; the tides are unfavorable, the bar in bad condition, the sea too high. Perhaps to-morrow or the next day.

I had almost had time to forget the difficulties and uncertainties of life in this place, — the perpetual anxiety in regard to the weather, the concern for this or that boat laden with soldiers or supplies, which is running some danger outside or which may founder on the bar; complications and dangers of all sorts connected with the disembarking of troops, — a thing which seems so simple when looked at from a distance, but which is surrounded by a world of difficulties in such places.

SATURDAY, November 3.

En route this morning for the squadron out on the open sea. At the end of a half hour the sinister shore of China disappears behind us, and the smoke-stacks of the iron-clads begin to pour forth their black smoke upon the horizon. We fear we shall have to turn back, the weather is so bad.

Dripping with fog, however, we arrive at last, and I jump aboard the *Redoutable*, where my comrades, with no taste of high life in China to break the monotony, have been at work for forty days.

Chapter V

Return to Ning-Hia

Six weeks later. A cold and gloomy morning. After having been at Tien-Tsin, Pekin, and other places, where so many strange and gloomy things have come to our notice, here we are back again at Ning-Hia, which we have had time to forget; our boat has gone back to its old moorings, and we return to the French fort.

It is cold and dull; autumn, which is so severe in these parts, has brought with it sudden frosts; the birches and willows have lost all their leaves, and the sky is cold and lowering.

The Zouaves who are living in the fort, and who came so light-heartedly only a month ago to take the place of our sailors, have already buried some of their number, who died of typhus or were shot. This very morning we have paid the last honors to two of them, killed by Russian balls in a particularly tragic manner, all the result of a mistake.

The sandy roads strewn with yellow leaves are solitary. The Cossacks have evacuated their camps and disappeared to the other side of the Great Wall, in the direction of Manchuria. The agitation of the earlier days is over; as well as the confusion and the joyous crowds; all have gone into winter quarters in the places assigned to them, and as the peasants of the vicinity have not returned, their villages are abandoned and empty.

The fort, though still ornamented with Chinese emblems, now bears a French name; it is called "Fort Admiral-Pottier."

As we entered trumpets resounded for the admiral, and the Zouaves, ranged under the guns, looked with respectful sorrow at their chief, who had just honored with his presence the funeral services of two soldiers.

As soon as we cross the threshold we feel quite unexpectedly as though we were on French soil; it would be hard to say by what spell these Zouaves have made of this place and its surroundings in one short month, something which is like a bit of home.

There have been no great changes; they have been content with removing Chinese filth, with putting the war supplies in order, with whitewashing their quarters, and with organizing a bakery where the bread has a good smell, and a hospital where the many wounded, alas, and the sick, sleep on very clean little camp beds. All this at once and quite inexplicably creates a feeling that one is in France again.

In the court of honor in the centre of the fort, in front of the door leading to the room where the mandarin is enthroned, two gun-carriages stand, unharnessed. Their wheels are decorated with leaves and they are covered over with white sheets, upon which are scattered poor little bouquets fastened on with pins. They are the last flowers from the neighboring Chinese gardens, — poor chrysanthemums and stunted roses touched by the frost, all arranged with touching care and kindly soldierly awkwardness, for the dead comrades who lie there on these carriages in coffins covered with the French flag.

It is a surprise to find this vast mandarin's room transformed by the Zouaves into a chapel. A strange chapel truly! On the whitewashed walls the vests of Chinese soldiers are fastened up and arranged like trophies with sabres and poniards, while the candlesticks that stand on the white altar-cloth are made of shell and bayonets, — thus naïvely and charmingly does the soldier know how to manage when he is in exile.

A military mass begins with trumpet blasts that make the Zouaves fall upon their knees; mass is said by the chaplain of the squadron, in mourning dress, — a mass for the dead, for the two who are asleep on the wagons near the door decorated with late flowers. From the court Bach's Prelude, played on muffled brass, rises like a prayer, the dominant note in this mingling of home and foreign land, of funeral service and gray morning.

Then they depart for a near-by enclosure which we have turned into a cemetery. Mules are harnessed to the heavy gun-carriages, the admiral himself leading the procession along the sandy paths where the Zouaves form a double row, presenting arms.

The sun does not pierce the autumn clouds that lower this morning over the burial of these children of France. It is cold and gloomy, and the birches and willows of the desolate country continue to drop their leaves upon us.

This improvised cemetery, surrounded by so much that is exotic, has also taken on a French air, — no doubt because of the brave home names inscribed on wooden crosses that mark the new-made graves; because of pots of chrysanthemums brought by comrades to these sad mounds of earth. And yet just beyond the wall which protects our dead, that other wall which rises and is indefinitely prolonged into the gray November country, is the Great Wall of China; and we are in exile far, frightfully far from home.

Now the coffins have been lowered, each one to its hole, adding to the already long row of newmade graves; all the Zouaves approach in serried rank while their commandant recalls in a few words how these two fell.

"It was not far from here. The company was marching without suspicion in the direction of a fort from which the Russian flag had just been hoisted, when suddenly balls began to rain like hail. The Russians behind their ramparts were new-comers who had not seen the Zouaves, and who mistook their red hats for the caps of the Boxers. Before they recognized their mistake several of our men lay on the ground; seven, one of them a captain, were wounded, and these two were dead. One of them was the sergeant who waved our flag in an effort to stop the firing."

Then the admiral addresses the Zouaves, whose eyes, all in a row, are filled with tears; and as he steps forward upon the pile of loose earth so that he may reach the graves with his sword, and says to those who lie there, "I salute you as soldiers for the last time," a real sob is audible, heartfelt, and unrestrained, from the breast of a big hearty fellow who looks to be not the least brave among those in the ranks.

Beside all this, how pitifully, how ironically empty are many of the pompous ceremonies at official burials with their fine discourses!

In these times of weakness and mediocrity, when nothing is sacred and the future is full of fear, happy are they who are cut down where they stand; happy are they who, young and pure, fall for the sake of adorable dreams of country and of honor, who are borne away wrapped in the modest flag of their country and greeted as soldiers with simple words that bring tears to the eyes.

Chapter VI

Pekin in Springtime

I
THURSDAY, April 18, 1901.

THE TERRIBLE CHINESE winter which has pursued us for four months in this ice-filled gulf of Pekin is over, and here we are again at our wretched post, having returned with the spring to the thick and yellow waters at the mouth of the Pei-Ho.

To-day wireless telegraphy, by a series of imperceptible vibrations gathered at the top of the *Redoutable's* mast, informs us that the palace of the Empress, occupied by Field-Marshal von Waldersee, was burned last night, and that the German chief-of-staff perished in the flames.

We were the only ones of all the allied squadrons who received this notice, and the admiral at once ordered me to depart for Pekin to offer his condolences, and to represent him at the funeral ceremonies.

There was just twenty-five minutes for my preparations, for the packing of luggage, great and small; for the boat which must take me ashore cannot wait without risk of missing the tide, and so being unable to cross the bar of the river to-night. At the end of an hour my foot is on the soil of horrible Taku, near the French quarter, where I must spend the night.

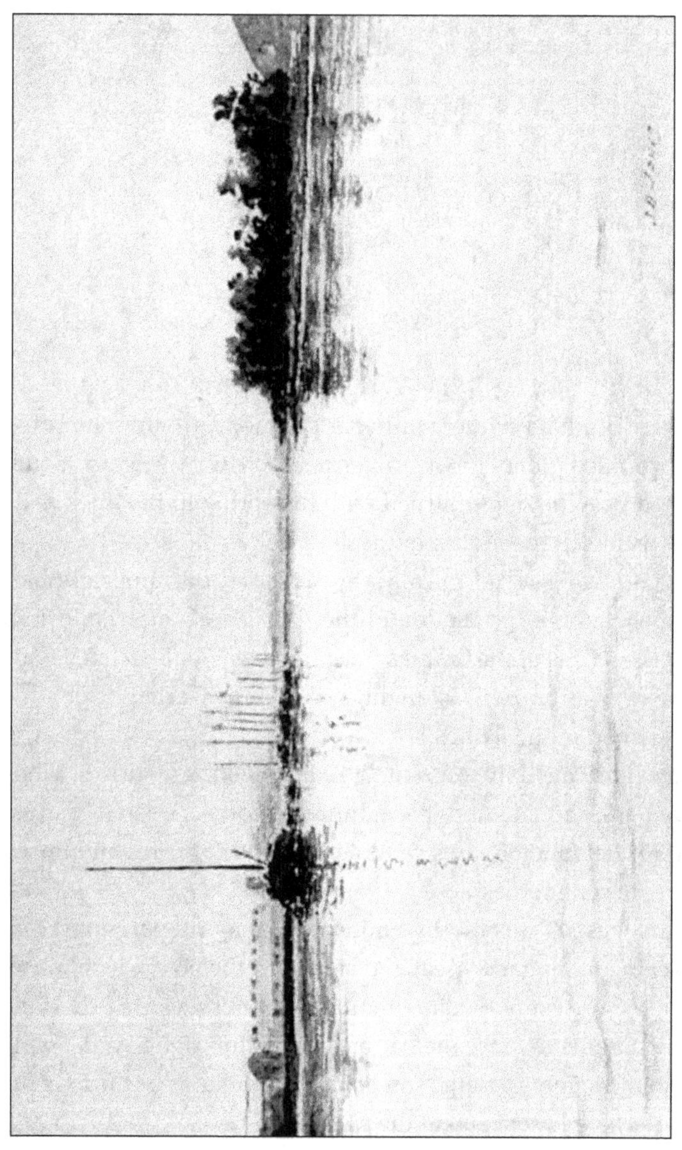

FRIDAY, April 19.

The railway destroyed by the Boxers has been rebuilt, and the train which I take this morning goes straight to Pekin, arriving there about four o'clock this afternoon, — a rapid and commonplace journey, very different from the one I made at the beginning of winter by junk and on horseback.

The spring rains have not begun; the chill verdure of May, the sorghos and the young willows, later than they are in our climate, emerge with great difficulty from the dry soil and cast a hesitating shadow upon the Chinese plains, powdered with gray dust and burned by an already torrid sun.

And how different is the appearance of Pekin! The first time we approached it, not by the superhuman ramparts of the Tartar City, but by those of the Chinese City, less imposing and less sombre.

To my surprise the train passes right through a fresh breach in the wall, enters the heart of the town, and lands one at the door of the Temple of Heaven. It seems that it is the same with the line from Pao-Ting-Fou; the Babylonian enclosure has been pierced, and the railroad enters Pekin and comes to an end only at the imperial quarters. What unheard-of changes the Celestial Emperor will find if he ever returns! — locomotives whistling and running right through this old capital of stability and decay.

On the platform of the temporary station there was an almost joyous animation, and many Europeans, too, were on hand to meet the incoming travellers.

Among the numerous officers who were there is one whom I recognize, although I never have seen him, and toward whom I advance spontaneously, — Colonel Marchand, the well-known hero, who arrived in Pekin last November, after I had left. We take a carriage together bound for the French quarter, where I am to be entertained.

The general quarters are a league away, still in the small Palace of the North, which was known to me in its Chinese splendor, and of whose earlier transformations I was a witness. The colonel himself lives near by in the Rotunda Palace, and we discover in the course of conversation that he has chosen for his private dwelling the same kiosk which I used for my work-room last season.

We make the trip by way of the grand avenue used by processions and emperors, through the triple gates in the colossal red walls under the murderous dungeon; over the marble bridges between great grinning marble lions, and between ivory-colored obelisks surmounted by animals out of dreamland.

And when, after the jolting, the noise, and the crowds, our carriage glides at last over the large paving-stones of the Yellow City, all this magnificence seems to me, on second sight, more than ever condemned, — a thing which has had its day. Imperial Pekin, in its everlasting dust, is now warmed by the rays of the April sun, yet it does not waken, does not return to life after its long, cold winter. Not a drop of rain has fallen yet, the ground is dust, the parks are dust.

The old cedars, black and powdery, seem like the mummies of trees, whilst the green of the monotonous willows is just beginning to appear in the terrible ashen-white sunshine.

The highest roofs rise toward a clear sky which is a mixture of heat and light, — pyramids of gold-colored faience whose age and dilapidation are more evident than ever amid the green and the birds'-nests. The Chinese storks have come back with the spring, and are perched in rows along the highest parts of the great roofs, on the precious tiles, among the horns and claws and enamelled monsters; they are small, motionless white creatures, — half lost in the dazzling whiteness of the sky, — who seem to be meditating on the destruction of the city as they contemplate the dismal dwellings at their feet. Really I find that Pekin has aged since autumn, aged a century or two; the April sunshine emphasizes all this and classes it definitely among the hopeless ruins. One feels that its end has come, and that there is no possible resurrection for it.

SATURDAY, April 20.

The funeral of General Schwarzhof, one of the greatest enemies of France, took place at nine o'clock this morning under a torrid sun; he came to a most unexpected end here in this Chinese palace just as he seemed about to become quartermaster-general of the German army.

The entire palace was not burned, only that superb part where he and the marshal lived, the apartments with the incomparable ebony woodwork and the throne room filled with *chefs-d'œuvre* of ancient art.

The casket has been placed in one of the great rooms left untouched by the fire. In front of the doorway the white-haired marshal stands in the dangerous sunshine. Somewhat overcome, but preserving the exquisite grace of a gentleman and a soldier, he receives the officers who are presented to him, — officers from all countries in every kind of dress, who arrive on horseback, on foot, and in carriages, in cocked hats and in helmets decorated with wings or with feathers. Timid Chinese dignitaries who seem to belong to another world and another age of human history come also; and gentlemen high in the diplomatic service are not lacking, brought here, by some anachronism, in old Asiatic palanquins.

The Chinese character of the room is entirely concealed by branches of cypress and cedar, gathered from the imperial park by the German soldiers and by our own; they cover the walls and ceiling and are strewn over the floor, exhaling a balsamic odor of the forest around the casket, which is half hidden by white lilacs from the Empress's garden.

After the address by a Lutheran pastor, there is a chorus from Händel, sung from behind the branches by some young German soldiers with voices so pure and fresh that they are as restful as music from heaven. Tame pigeons, whose habits have been interfered with by the invasion of barbarians, fly tranquilly above our plumed and gilded heads.

At the sound of the military brasses the procession begins to move, to make the tour of the Lake of the Lotus. All along the road a hedge, such as was never seen before, is formed by the soldiers of all nations; Bavarians are followed by Cossacks, Italians by Japanese, etc. Among so many rather sombre uniforms the red waistcoats of the small English detachment stand out sharply, and their reflections in the lake are like cruel and bloody trails. It is a very small detachment, almost ridiculously so beside those that other countries have sent; — England is represented in China chiefly by Indian hordes, every one knows, alas, with what a task her troops are elsewhere occupied at the present moment.

The images of the lines of soldiers are reflected inversely in the water as well as the great desolate palaces, the marble quays, and the faience kiosks, built here and there among the trees; in certain places the lotus, which is beginning to come up from the slimy mud, shows above the surface its first leaves, of a green tinged with pink.

A stop is made at a dark pagoda, where the coffin is temporarily left. This pagoda is so surrounded with foliage that it seems at first as though one were simply entering a garden of cedars, willows, and white lilacs; but soon the eye distinguishes behind and above this verdure other rarer and more magnificent foliage, carved by the Chinese for their gods in the form of clusters of maple or of bamboo, which form under the ceiling a high arbor of gold.

And here this curious funeral comes to an end. The groups divide, sorting themselves according to nations, and soon disperse among the hot wooded walks in the direction of their various palaces.

The setting of the Yellow City seems vaster, more extensive than ever in the April light. One is bewildered by so much artificiality. How marvellous the genius of these people has been! To have created bodily, in the midst of an arid plain, a lifeless desert, a city twenty leagues in circumference, with aqueducts, woods, rivers, mountains, and lakes! To have created forest distances and watery horizons, to give their sovereigns illusions of freshness! And to have enclosed all this, — which in itself is so large that one cannot see its boundaries, — to have separated it from the rest of the world, to have sequestered it, if one may use the word, behind such formidable walls!

What their most audacious architects have not been able to create, nor their proudest emperors, is a real springtime in this parched land, — a spring like ours, with its warm rains and its tremendously rapid growth of grass, ferns, and flowers. Here there is no turf, no moss, no odorous hay; the springtime resurrection is indicated here by the thin foliage on the willows, by tufts of grass here and there, or by the blossoming of a sort of purple gillyflower that springs up out of the dusty soil. It rains only in June, and then there is a deluge flooding all things.

Poor Yellow City, where we walk this morning, meeting so many people, so many armed detachments, so many uniforms; poor Yellow City, closed to the world for so many centuries, an inviolable refuge for the rites and mysteries of the past; city of splendor, oppression, and silence! When I saw it in the autumn it had an air of desertion which suited it; but now I find it overrun by the soldiers of all Europe. In all the palaces and golden pagodas "barbarian" troopers drag their swords or groom their horses under the very noses of the great dreamy Buddhas.

I saw to-day, at a Chinese merchant's, a collection of the ingenious terra-cotta statuettes, which are a specialty of Tien-Tsin. Up to the present year, only inhabitants of the Celestial Empire have been represented, — people of all social conditions and in every circumstance of life; but these, inspired by the invasion, represent various Occidental warriors, whose types and costumes are reproduced with astonishing accuracy. The modellers have given to the soldiers of certain European countries, which I prefer not to designate, an expression of fierce rage, and have placed in their hands light swords or bludgeons, or whips raised as if to strike a blow.

Our own men wear the red cap of the country, and are exceedingly French as to faces, with moustaches made of yellow or brown silk; each one carries tenderly in his arms a little Chinese baby. They are posed in different ways, but all are inspired by the same idea; the little Chinese is sometimes holding the soldier by the neck and embracing him; sometimes the soldier is tossing the laughing child, or, again, he is carefully wrapping it in his winter cloak. Thus it is, in the eyes of these careful observers, that while others are rough and always ready to strike a blow, our soldier is the one who after the battle becomes the big brother of the enemy's little children; after several months of practically living together, the Chinese have chosen this, and this alone, to characterize the French.

Examples of these various statuettes ought to be scattered broadcast throughout Europe: the comparison would be for us a glorious trophy to bring back from the war, and would close the mouths of numerous imbeciles in our own country[2].

---

2 A few days later, by order of the superior officers, those accusing statues were withdrawn from the market and the models destroyed. Only the statuettes of the French remained on sale, and they have become very rare.

In the afternoon Marshal von Waldersee came to our headquarters. He was kind enough to say, what was in fact the truth, that the fire was extinguished almost entirely by our soldiers, led by my friend Colonel Marchand.

About eleven o'clock, on the evening of the fire, the colonel was dreaming on the high terrace of the Rotunda Palace, in a favorable spot from which to see the great red jet shoot superbly up from the mass of sculptured ebony and fine lacquer, as well as its reflection in the water. He was the first to reach the spot with a few of our men, and he was able to keep ten fire-engines going until morning, while our marines, under his orders, chopped down some of the blazing parts. It was owing to him, also, that they were able to recover General Schwarzhof's body. He constantly directed a stream of water toward the spot where he knew he had fallen, in default of which incineration would have been complete.

This evening I go to call on Monsignor Favier, who has just returned from his trip to Europe, full of confidence in his plans.

How changed is all connected with the Catholic concession since the autumn! Instead of silence and destruction all is life and activity. Eight hundred workmen — almost all Boxers, the bishop says with a defiant smile — are at work repairing the cathedral, which is encased from top to bottom in bamboo scaffoldings. The avenues about it have been widened and planted with rows of young acacias, and countless improvements have been undertaken, as though an era of peace had begun and persecutions were over forever.

While I am conversing with the bishop in the white parlor, the marshal arrives. He naturally refers again to the burning of his palace, and with delicate courtesy informs us that of all the souvenirs which he lost in the disaster the one he most regrets is the Cross of the Legion of Honor.

II

SUNDAY, April 21.

MY EASY MISSION over, there is nothing for me to do but to return to the *Redoutable*.

But the general is kind enough to invite me to remain with him for a few days. He proposes that we pay a visit to the tombs of the emperors of the present dynasty, which are in a sacred wood about fifty miles southwest of Pekin, — tombs which never had been seen before this war, and which probably never will be seen after it is over. In order to accomplish this it is necessary to write in advance to warn the mandarins, and especially the commandants of the French posts stationed along the route, and there is quite an expedition to organize. So I asked the admiral for ten days, which he kindly granted me by telegraph, and am still here, a guest of the palace for much longer than I expected.

This Sunday morning I go over to Monsignor's cathedral to take part in the grand mass for the Chinese.

I enter at the left of the nave, which is the side for men, while the right side is reserved for women.

When I arrive the church is already packed with Chinese, both men and women, kneeling close together, and humming in an undertone a sort of uninterrupted chant that resembles the buzzing of an immense hive. There is a strong smell of musk, for both cotton and silk robes are saturated with it; and besides that there is the intolerable odor that belongs to the yellow race, and which is something indescribable. In front of me, to the farthest ends of the church, men with bowed heads are kneeling.

I see backs by the hundreds with long queues hanging over them. On the women's side are bright silks, — a perfect medley of colors; chignons, smooth and black as varnished ebony, with flowers and gold pins. Everybody sings with mouths almost closed, as if in a dream. Their devotion is obvious, and it is touching, in spite of the extreme drollery of the people; they really pray, and seem to do so with fervor and humility.

Now comes the spectacle for which I confess I came, — the coming out from mass, — a great opportunity to see some of the beautiful ladies of Pekin, for they do not show themselves in the street, where only women of the lower classes walk about.

There were several hundred elegant women who slowly came out, one after another, their feet too small and their shoes too high. Oh, the line of strange little painted faces and the finery that emerged from that narrow doorway! The cut of the pantaloons, the cut of the tunics, the combination of forms and colors, must be as old as China, and how far it seems from us! They are like dolls of another age, another world, who have escaped from old parasols or decorated jars, to take on reality and life this beautiful April morning. Among them are Chinese ladies with deformed toes and incredibly small, pointed shoes; their stiff, heavy masses of hair are pointed too, and arranged at the nape of the neck like birds' tails. There are Tartar ladies, belonging to the special aristocracy known as "the eight banners;" their feet are natural, but their embroidered slippers have stilt-like heels; their hair is long, and is wound like a skein of black silk on a piece of board placed crosswise back of their heads, so that it forms two horizontal cones with an artificial flower at each end.

They paint themselves like the wax figures at the hairdressers', — white, with a bright pink spot in the middle of each cheek; one feels that it is done according to custom and etiquette, without the least attempt at creating an illusion.

They chatter and laugh discreetly; they lead by the hand the most adorable babies (who were as good as little porcelain kittens during mass), decked out, and their hair dressed in the most comical fashion. Many of the women are pretty, very pretty; almost all seem decent, reserved, and *comme il faut.*

The exit from the church was accomplished quietly, with every appearance of peace and happiness, in complete confidence in these surroundings so recently the scene of massacre and other horrors. The gates of the enclosure are wide open, and a new avenue, bordered by young trees, has been laid out over what was not long since a charnel-house.

A great number of little Chinese carts, upholstered in beautiful silk or in blue cotton, are waiting, their heavy wheels decorated with copper; all the dolls get in with much ceremony, and depart as though they were leaving some festive performance.

Once more the Christians in China have won a victory, and they triumph generously — until the next massacre.

At two o'clock to-day, as is the Sunday custom, the marine band plays in the court at headquarters, — in the court of the Palace of the North, which I had known filled with strange and magnificent débris in a cold autumn wind, but which at present is all cleared up as neat as a pin, with the April green beginning to show on the branches of the little trees.

This semblance of a French Sunday is rather sad. The feeling of exile which one never loses here is made all the keener by the poor music, to which there are but few listeners; no dressy women or happy babies, just two or three groups of idle soldiers and a few of the sick or wounded from the hospital, their young faces pale and wan, one dragging a limb, another leaning on a crutch.

And yet there are moments when it does suggest home; the going and coming of the marines and of the good Sisters reminds one of some little corner of France; beyond the glass galleries which surround this court rises the slender Gothic tower of the neighboring church, with a large tricolored flag floating from the top, high up in the blue sky, dominating everything, and protecting the little country we have improvised here in the haunts of the Chinese emperors.

What a change has taken place in this Palace of the North since my stay here last autumn.

With the exception of the part reserved for the general and his officers, all the galleries and all the dependencies have become hospital wards for our soldiers. They are admirably adapted to this purpose, for they are separated from one another by courts, and stand on high foundations of granite. There are two hundred beds for the poor sick soldiers, who are most comfortably installed in them, with light and air at pleasure, thanks to the way this fantastic palace is built. The good Sisters with their white pointed caps move about with short, quick steps, distributing medicines, clean linen, and smiles.

A small parlor is set apart for the head-nurse, — an elderly woman, with a fine, wrinkled face, who has just received the cross, in the presence of all the troops, for her admirable services during the siege. Her little whitewashed parlor is altogether typical and charming, with its six Chinese chairs, its Chinese table, its two Chinese watercolors of flowers and fruits that hang on the wall, — all chosen from amongst the most modest of the Sardanapalian reserves of the Empress; added to these is a large plaster image of the Virgin, enthroned in the place of honor, between two jars filled with white lilacs.

White lilacs! The most magnificent bunches of them grow in all the walled gardens of this palace; they are the sole joyful signs of April, of real spring under this burning sun; and they are a boon to the Sisters, who make regular thickets of them in honor of the Virgin and saints, on their simple altars.

I had known all these mandarins' and gardeners' houses, which extend on among the trees, in complete disarray, filled with strange spoils, filth, and pestilential smells; now they are clean and whitewashed, with nothing disagreeable about them.

The nuns have established here a wash-house, there a kitchen where good broth is made for the invalids, or a linen room, where piles of cleansmelling sheets and shirts for the sick are ranged on shelves covered with immaculate papers.

Like the simplest of our sailors or soldiers, I am very much inclined to be charmed and comforted by the mere sight of a good Sister's cap. It is no doubt an indication of a regrettable lack in my imagination, but I have much less of a thrill when I look upon the head-dress of a lay nurse.

Outside of our quarters, in these unheard-of times for Pekin, Sunday is marked by the great numbers of soldiers of all countries who are circulating about its streets.

The city has been divided into districts, each placed under the care of one of the invading peoples, and the different zones mingle very little with one another; the officers occasionally, the soldiers almost never. As an exception, the Germans come to us sometimes, and we go to them, for one of the undeniable results of this war has been to establish a sympathy between the men of the two armies; but the international relations of our troops are limited to this one exception.

The part of Pekin that fell to France — several kilometres in circumference — is the one where the Boxers destroyed most during the siege, the one that is most ruined and solitary, but also the one to which life and confidence soonest returned. Our soldiers take kindly to the Chinese, both men and women, and even to the babies. They have made friends everywhere, as may be seen by the way the Chinese approach them instead of running away.

In the French part of Pekin every little house flies the tricolor as a safeguard. Many of the people have even pasted on their doors placards of white paper, obtained through the kind offices of some of our men, on which may be read in big, childish handwriting: "We are Chinese protected by French" or "Here we are all Chinese Christians."

And every little baby, naked or clothed, with his ribbon and his queue, has learned, smilingly, to make the military salute as we pass.

At sunset the soldiers turn in, the barracks are closed. Silence and darkness everywhere.

The night is particularly dark. About two o'clock I leave my quarters with one of my comrades of the land force. Lantern in hand, we set forth in the dark labyrinth; challenged at first here and there by sentinels, then, meeting no one but frightened dogs, we cross ruins, cesspools, and wretched streets that breathe death.

A very dubious-looking house is our goal. The watchmen at the gate, who were on the lookout, announce us by a long, sinister cry, and we plunge into a series of winding passageways and dark recesses. Then come several small rooms with low ceilings, which are stuffy, and lighted only by dim, smoky lamps; their furnishings consist of a divan and an arm-chair; the air, which is scarcely breathable, is saturated with opium and musk. The patron and the patroness have both the *embonpoint* and the patriarchal good nature which go along with such a house.

I beg that my reader will not misunderstand me; this is a *house of song* (one of the oldest of Chinese institutions, now tending to disappear), and one comes here simply to listen to music, surrounded by clouds of overpowering smoke.

Hesitatingly we take our places in one of the small rooms, on a red couch covered with red cushions embroidered with natural representations of wild animals. Its cleanliness is dubious and the excessive odors disturb us. On the papered walls hang water-colors representing beatified sages among the clouds. In one corner an old German clock, which must have been in Pekin at least a hundred years, ticks a shrill tick-tock. It seems as though from the moment of our arrival our minds were affected by the heavy opium dreams that have been evolved on this divan under the restraint of the oppressive dark ceilings; and yet this is an elegant resort for the Chinese, a place apart, to which, before the war, no amount of money would admit any European.

Pushing aside the long, poisonous pipes that are offered us, we light some Turkish cigarettes, and the music begins.

The first to appear is a guitarist, and as marvellous a one as could be found at Granada or Seville. He makes his strings weep songs of infinite sadness.

Afterwards, for our amusement, he imitates on his guitar the sound of a French regiment passing, the muffled drums and the trumpets in the distance playing the "March of the Zouaves."

Finally, three little old women appear, stout and rather pale, who are to give us some plaintive trios with minor strains that correspond with the dreams that follow opium smoking. But before beginning, one of the three, who is the star, — a curious, very much dressed little creature, with a tiara of rice-paper flowers, like a goddess, — advances toward me on the toes of her tortured feet, extends her hand to me in European fashion, and says in French, with a Creole accent, and not without a certain distinction of manner, "Good evening, colonel."

It was the last thing I expected! Certainly the occupation of Pekin by French troops has been prolific in unexpected results.

MONDAY, April 22.

My journey to the Tombs of the Emperors takes some time to organize. The replies that come to headquarters state that the country has been less safe for the past few days, that bands of Boxers have appeared in the province, and they are waiting further instructions before consenting to my departure.

In the meantime I make another visit in the hot spring sunshine to the horrors of the Christian cemeteries violated by the Chinese.

The confusion there is unchanged; there is the same chaos of melancholy marbles, of mutilated emblems, of steles fallen and broken. The human remains which the Boxers did not have time to destroy before they were routed lie in the same places; no pious hand has ventured to bury them again, for, according to Chinese ideas, it would be accepting the proffered injury to put them back in the ground; they must lie there, crying for vengeance, until the day of complete reparation. There is no change in this place of abomination, except that it is no longer frozen; the sun shines, and here and there yellow dandelions or violet gillyflowers are blossoming in the sandy soil.

As to the great yawning wells which had been filled with the bodies of the tortured, time has begun to do its work; the wind has blown the dust and dirt over them, and their contents have dried to such an extent that they now form a compact gray mass, although an occasional foot or hand or skull still protrudes above the rest.

In one of these wells, on the human crust that rises nearly to the top of the ground, lies the body of a poor Chinese baby, dressed in a torn little shirt and swathed in red cotton, — it is a recent corpse, hardly stiff as yet. No doubt it is a little girl, for the Chinese have the most atrocious scorn for girls; the Sisters pick them up like this along the roads every day, thrown while still alive upon some rubbish heap. So it was, no doubt, with this one. She may have been ill, or ill-favored, or simply one too many in a family. She lies there face downward, with extended arms and little doll-like hands. Her face, from which the blood has been running, is lying on the most frightful rubbish; a few of the feathers of a young sparrow lie on the back of her neck, over which the flies are meandering.

Poor little creature in her red woollen rags with her little hands outstretched! Poor little face hidden so that no one shall see it more before its final decomposition!

CHAPTER VII

THE TOMBS OF THE EMPERORS

I

PEKIN, Friday, April 26, 1901.

AT LAST THE day has come for my departure for the sacred wood which encloses the imperial tombs.

At seven o'clock in the morning I leave the Palace of the North, taking with me my last autumn's servants, Osman and Renaud, as well as four African riflemen and a Chinese interpreter. We start on horseback on animals chosen for the journey, which will be transported by rail whenever we are.

First, two or three kilometres across Pekin in the beautiful morning light, along great thoroughfares magnificent in their desolation, the route of pageants and of emperors; through the triple red gates, between lions of marble and obelisks of marble, yellow as old ivory.

Now the railway station — it is in the centre of the city at the foot of the wall of the second enclosure, for the Western barbarians dared to commit the sacrilege of piercing the ramparts in order to introduce their submersive system.

Men and horses go aboard. Then the train threads its way across the devastated Chinese City, and for three or four kilometres skirts the colossal gray wall of the Tartar City, which continues to unfold itself, always the same, with the same bastions, the same battlements, without a gate, without anything, to relieve its monotony and its immensity.

A breach in the outer wall casts us forth at last into the melancholy country.

And for three hours and a half it is a journey through the dust of the plain, past demolished stations, rubbish, ruins. According to the great plans of the allied nations, this line, which actually goes to Pao-Ting-Fu, is to be extended several hundred leagues, so as to unite Pekin and Hang-Chow, two enormous cities. It would thus become one of the great arteries of new China, scattering along its way the benefits of Occidental civilization.

At noon we alight at Tchou-Tchou, a great walled city, whose high battlemented ramparts and two twelve-storied towers are perceived as through a cloud of ashes. A man is scarcely recognizable at twenty paces, as in times of fog in the north, so filled with dust is the air; and the sun, though dimmed and yellow, reflects a heat that is overpowering.

The commandant and the officers of the French port, which has occupied Tchou-Tchou since the autumn, were kind enough to meet me and to take me for breakfast to their table in the comparative freshness of the big dark pagodas where they with their men were installed. The road to the tombs[3], they tell me, which latterly has seemed quite safe, has been less so for a few days, a band of two hundred marauding Boxers having yesterday attacked one of the large villages through which I must pass, where they fought all the morning, — until the appearance of a French detachment who came to the aid of the villagers sent the Boxers flying like a flock of sparrows.

"Two hundred Boxers," continued the commandant of the post, making a mental calculation; "let me see, two hundred Boxers: you will have to have at least ten men. You already have

---

3 The reference here is not to the tombs of the Mings, which have for many years been explored by all Europeans on their way to Pekin, but to the tombs of the emperors of the reigning dynasty, whose very approaches have always been forbidden.

six horsemen; I will, if you wish, add four more."

I felt that I ought to make some suitable acknowledgment, to reply that it was too much, that he overpowered me. Then under the eyes of the Buddhas, who were watching us breakfast, we both began to laugh, struck all at once by the air of extravagant bluster in what we were saying. In truth it had the force of

"Paraissez, Navarrois, Maures et Castillans;"

and yet, ten men against two hundred Boxers are really all that are necessary. They are tenacious and terrible only behind walls, those fellows; but in a flat country — it is highly probable, moreover, that I shall not see the queue of one. I accept the reinforcement, — four brave soldiers, who will be delighted to accompany me; I accept so much the more readily, since my expedition will thus take on the proportions of a military reconnaissance, and this, it appears, will be a good thing just now.

At two o'clock we remount our horses, for we are to sleep in an old walled town twenty-five kilometres farther on, called Lai-Chow-Chien (Chinese cities seem to claim these names; we know of one called Cha-Ma-Miaou, and another, a very large, ancient capital, Chien-Chien).

We make a plunge and disappear at once in a cloud of dust which the wind chases over the plain, — the immense, suffocating plain. There is no illusion possible; it is the "yellow wind" which has arisen, — a wind which generally blows in periods of three days, adding to the dust of China all that of the Mongolian desert.

No roads but deep tracks, paths several feet below the surface, which could only have been hollowed there in the course of centuries. A frightful country, which has, since the beginning of time, endured torrid heat and almost hyperborean cold. In this dry, powdery soil how can the new wheat grow, which here and there makes squares of really fresh green in the midst of the infinite grays? There are also from time to time a few sparse clumps of young elms and willows, somewhat different from ours, but nevertheless recognizable, just showing their first tiny leaves. Monotony and sadness; one would call it a poor landscape of the extreme north, lighted by an African sun, — a sun that has mistaken the latitude.

At a turn of the crooked road a band of laborers who see us suddenly spring up, are frightened, and throw down their spades to run away. But one of them stops the others, crying, "Fanko pink" (French soldiers). "They are French, do not be afraid." Then they bend again over the burning earth, and peaceably continue their work, looking at us as we pass by from the corners of their eyes. Their confidence speaks volumes on the somewhat exceptional kind of "barbarians" our brave soldiers have known how to be, in the course of a European invasion.

The few clumps of willows scattered over the plains almost always shelter under their sparse foliage the villages of tillers of the soil, — little houses of clay and of gray brick, absurd little pagodas, which are crumbling in the sunshine. Warned by watchmen, men and children come out as we pass to look at us in silence with naïve curiosity; bare to the waist, very yellow, very thin, and very muscular; pantaloons of the ever similar dark blue cotton. Out of politeness each one uncoils and allows to hang down his back his long plaited hair, for to keep it on the crown of the head would be a disrespect to me. No women; they remain concealed. These people must have much the same impression of us that the peasants of Gaul had when Attila, chief of the army, passed with his escort, except that they are less frightened. Everything about us is astonishing, — costumes, arms, and faces. Even my horse, which is an Arabian stallion, must seem to them a huge, unusual, superb animal beside their own little horses,

with their big rough heads.

The frail willows, through which the sunlight sifts upon the houses and tiny pagodas of these primitive lives, scatter over us their blossoms, like tiny feathers or little tufts of cotton-wool, which fall in a shower, and mingle with the never-ending dust.

On the plain, which now begins again, level and always the same, I keep two or three hundred metres in advance of my little armed troop, to avoid the excessive dust raised by the trot of the horses' feet; a gray cloud behind me when I turn around shows me that they are following. The "yellow wind" continues to blow; we are powdered with it to such an extent that our horses, our moustaches, our uniforms have become of the color of ashes.

Toward five o'clock the old walled town where we are to pass the night appears before us. From afar it is almost imposing in the midst of the plain, with its high crenellated ramparts so sombre in color. Near by, no doubt, it would show but ruin and decrepitude, like the rest of China.

A horseman, bringing along with him the inevitable cloud of dust, comes out to meet me. It is the officer commanding the fifty men of the marine infantry who have occupied Lai-Chou-Chien since October. He informs me that the general has had the kindly thought of having me announced as one of the great mandarins of Occidental letters, so the mandarin of the town is coming out to meet me with an escort, and he has called together the neighboring villages for a fête which he is preparing for me.

In fact, here the procession comes, from out the crumbling old gates, advancing through the wasted fields, with red emblems and music.

Now it stops to await me, ranged in two lines on each side of the road. And following the usual ceremonial, some one, a servant of the mandarin, comes forward, fifty feet in advance of the others, with a large red paper, which is the visiting-card of his master. He himself, the timid mandarin, awaits, standing, with the people of his house, having come down from his palanquin out of deference. I extend my hand without dismounting, as I have been told to do, after which, in a cloud of gray dust, we make our way toward the great walls, followed by my cavaliers, and preceded by the procession of honor with music and emblems.

At the head are two big red parasols, surrounded with a fall of silk like the canopies in a procession; than a fantastic black butterfly, as large as an owl with extended wings, which is carried at the end of a stick by a child; then two rows of banners; then shields of red lacquered wood inscribed with letters of gold. As soon as we begin to march gongs commence to sound lugubriously at regular intervals as for a military salute, whilst heralds with prolonged cries announce my arrival to the inhabitants of the village.

Here we are at the gate, which seems like the entrance to a cavern; on each side are hung five or six little wooden cages, each one containing a kind of black beast, motionless in the midst of a swarm of flies; their tails may be seen hanging outside the bars like dead things. What can it be that keeps itself rolled up like a ball, and has such a long tail? Monkeys? Ah, horrors, they are heads that have been severed from their bodies! Each one of these pretty cages contains a human head, beginning to grow black in the sunshine, with long, braided hair which has been intentionally uncoiled.

We are swallowed up by the big gate, and are received by the inevitable grinning old granite monsters which at right and at left raise their great heads with the squinting eyes. Motionless, against the inner wall of the tunnel, the people press to see me pass, huddled together, climbing one upon the other, — yellow nakedness, blue cotton rags, ugly faces. The dust fills and obscures this vaulted passage where men and horses press,

ARTILLERIE
BATTERIE
DE
O CAMPAGNE

enveloped in the same gloom.

We have entered old provincial China, belonging to another era entirely unknown to us.

II

Ruin and dilapidation within the walls, as I expected, not from any fault of the Boxers or of the Allies, for the war did not come near here, but as a result of decay, of the falling into dust of this old China, our elder by more than thirty centuries.

The gong in front of me continues to sound lugubriously at fixed intervals, and the heralds continue to announce me to the people by prolonged cries, resounding through the little powdery streets under the still burning evening sun. One sees unused land and cultivated fields. Here and there granite monsters, defaced, shapeless, half buried, worn by years, indicate what was formerly the entrance to a palace.

Before a door which surmounts a tricolored pavilion the procession stops, and I dismount. For seven or eight months our fifty soldiers of the marine infantry have been quartered here, spending a whole long winter at Lai-Chou-Chien, separated from the rest of the world by snow and icy steppes, and leading a Crusoe-like existence in the midst of the most perplexing surroundings.

It is a surprise and a joy to come among them, to see again their honest home faces, after all the yellow ones we have met along the road, darting sharp enigmatical glances at us. This French quarter is like a bit of life, gaiety, and youth in the midst of mummified old China.

It is plain that the winter has been good for our soldiers, for the look of health is on their cheeks. They have organized themselves with a comical and somewhat marvellous ingenuity, creating lavatories, douche rooms, a schoolroom where they teach French to the little Chinese, and even a theatre. Living in intimate comradeship with the people of the town, who will before long be unwilling to see them go, they cultivate vegetable gardens, raise chickens and sheep, and bring up little ravens by hand like orphan babies.

It is arranged that I should sleep at the house of the mandarin after having supped at the French post. So at nine o'clock they come for me to conduct me to the "Yamen" with lanterns of state, decorated in a very Chinese fashion and as big as barrels.

The Chinese Yamen is always of tremendous extent. In the cool night air, picking my way by the light of lanterns, amongst huge stones and between rows of servants, I pass through a series of courts two hundred metres long, with I don't know how many ruined porticoes and peristyles with shaky steps, before reaching the crumbling and dusty lodging which the mandarin intends for me, — a separate building in the midst of a sort of yard, and surrounded by old trees with shapeless trunks. There, under the smoky rafters, I have a great room, with whitewashed walls, containing in the centre a platform with seats like a throne, also some heavy ebony arm-chairs; and as wall decorations some rolls of silk spread out, on which poetry, in Manchou characters, is written. In the wing on the left is a small bedroom for my two servants, and on the right one for me with window-panes of rice paper. On a platform is a very hard bed with covers of red silk, and, lastly, an incense burner, in which little sticks of incense are burning. All this is rural, naïve, and superannuated, antiquated even for China.

My timid host, in ceremonial costume, awaits me at the entrance, and makes me take a seat with him on the central throne, where he offers me the obligatory tea in porcelain a hundred years old. Then he had the discretion to bring the audience to a close and to bid me good-night. As he withdrew he told me not to be disturbed if I heard a good deal of coming and going over my head, as the space above was frequented by rats. Neither was I to be disturbed if I heard on the other side of my paper window-panes people walking up and down in the yard playing castanets; they would be the night watchmen, thus informing me that they were not asleep, and were doing their duty.

"There are many brigands in this country," he added; "the city with its high walls closes its gates at sunset, but the workmen going to the fields before daybreak have made a hole in the ramparts, — this the brigands have discovered, and do not hesitate to enter by it."

When this deep-bowing mandarin was gone, and I was alone in the darkness of my dwelling, in the heart of an isolated city whose gates were guarded by human heads in cages, I felt myself at an infinite distance away, separated from my own world by immense space as well as by time, by ages; it seemed to me that I was going to sleep amongst a people at least a thousand years behind our era.

SATURDAY, April 27.

The crowing of cocks, the singing of little birds on my roof, awoke me in my strange old room; and by the light that came in through my paper panes I guessed that the warm sun was shining out of doors.

Osman and Renaud, who were up before me, came to tell me that they were hurriedly making great preparations in the courtyard of the Yamen in order to give me a fête, a morning fête, because we had to continue our route to the imperial tombs soon after the mid-day meal.

It began about nine o'clock. I was given a seat in an arm-chair beside the mandarin, who seemed weighed down beneath his silken gowns. In front of me, in the dazzling sunshine, was the series of courts with porticoes of irregular outline and old monsters on pedestals. A crowd of Chinese — always the men alone, it is understood — have assembled in their eternal blue rags. The yellow wind which had died down at night, as usual, begins to blow again, and to whiten the heavens with dust. The acacias and the monotonous willows, which are almost the only trees scattered over this northern China, show here and there on their slender old branches little pale-green leaves just barely out.

First comes the slow, the very slow, passing of a band with many gongs, cymbals, and bells all muffled; the melody seems to be carried by a sweet, melancholy, and persistent unison of flutes, — large flutes, with a deep tone, some of which have several tubes, and resemble sheaves of wheat. It is sweet and lulling, exquisite to hear.

Now the musicians seat themselves near us, in a circle, to open the fête. All at once the rhythm changes, grows more rapid, and becomes a dance. Then from afar, from the retirement of the courts and the old porticoes, one sees above the heads of the crowd, through the dust that grows thicker and thicker, a troop of dancing creatures two or three times taller than men, swinging along, swinging in regular time and playing citherns, fanning themselves, and comporting themselves generally in an exaggerated, nervous epileptic manner. — Giants? Jumping Jacks? What can they be? They are approaching rapidly with long, leaping steps, and here they are in front of us. Ah, they are on stilts, enormously high stilts. They are taller on their wooden legs than the shepherds of the Landes, and they hop like big grasshoppers. They are in costume and made up, — painted, rouged. They have wigs, false beards; they represent gods, genii such as one sees on old pagodas; they represent princesses also, with beautiful robes of embroidered silk, with cheeks too

pink and white, and with artificial flowers in their chignons, —
princesses all very tall, fanning themselves in an exaggerated
way, and swinging along like the rest of the company, with
the same regular, continuous movement, as persistent as the
pendulum of a clock.

All these stilt-walkers, it seems, are merely young men of
a neighboring village, who have formed themselves into a
gymnastic society, and who do this for amusement. In the smallest
villages in the interior of China, centuries, yes, thousands of years,
before the custom reached us, the men — fathers and sons —
began to devote themselves passionately to feats of strength and
skill, founding rival societies, some becoming acrobats, others
balancers, or jugglers, and organizing contests. It is especially
during the long winters that they exercise, when all is frozen,
and when each little human group must live alone in the midst
of a desert of snow.

In fact, in spite of their white wigs and their centenarian
beards, it is obvious that all these people are young, very young,
with childlike smiles. They smile naïvely, these droll, pleasant
princesses with the over-long legs, whose fan motions are so
excited and who dance more and more disjointedly, bending,
reversing, and shaking their heads and their bodies in a frenzy.
They smile naïvely, these old men with children's faces; they play
the cithern or the tambourine as though they were possessed.
The persistent unison of the flutes seems to bewitch them, to put
them into a special condition of madness, expressed by more and
more convulsive movements.

At a given signal each one stands on a single stilt, the other
leg raised, the second stilt thrown back over the shoulder; and
by prodigies of balancing they dance harder than ever, like
marionettes whose springs are out of order, whose mechanism
is about to break down. Then bars two metres high are brought

in, and they jump over them, every one taking part, including the princesses, the old men, and the genii, all keeping up an incessant play of fans and a beating of tambourines.

At last, when they can hold out no longer and go and lean against the porticoes among the old acacias and willows, another company just like the first comes forward and begins again, to the same tune, a similar dance. They represent the same persons, the same genii, the same long-bearded gods, the same beautiful mincing dames. In their accoutrements, so unknown to us, and with their curiously wrinkled faces, these dancers are the incarnation of ancient mythological dreams dreamed long ago in the dark ages by human beings at an infinite distance from us; and these customs are handed down from generation to generation, and from one end of the country to the other in that unchanging way in which rites, forms, and property in China are invariably transmitted.

This fête, this dance, extremely novel as it is, retains its village, its rustic character, and is as simple as any truly rural entertainment.

They finally cease jumping the bars, and now two terrible beasts come forth, one red and one green. They are big, heraldic dragons at least twenty metres long, with the raised heads, the yawning mouths, the horns, and claws, and horrible squinting eyes that everybody knows. They advance rapidly, throwing themselves onto the shoulders of the crowd with the undulations of a reptile; they are light, however, made of pasteboard, covered with some sort of stuff, and each beast is supported in the air by means of sticks, by a dozen skilful young men who have a subtle knack of giving to their movements a serpentine effect. A sort of master of the ballet precedes them, holding in his hand a ball which they never lose sight of, and which he uses as the leader of an orchestra uses his baton, to guide the writhings of the monsters.

The two great creatures content themselves with dancing before me, to the sound of flutes and gongs, in the centre of the circle of Chinese, which is extended in order to make room for them. At length the struggle becomes quite terrible, while the gongs and cymbals rage. They become entangled, they roll on top of one another, they drag their long rings in the dust, and then, all at once, with a bound they get up, as though in a passion, and stand shaking their enormous heads at one another, trembling with rage. The ballet master, nervously moving his director's ball, throws himself about and rolls his ferocious eyes.

The dust on the crowd grows thicker and thicker, and on the invisible dragon-bearers; it rises in clouds, rendering this battle between the red beast and the green beast almost fantastic. The sun burns as in a tropical country, and yet the sad Chinese April, anæmic from such a drought following the frozen winter, is barely heralded by the tender color of the few tiny leaves on the old willows and acacias of the court.

After breakfast some of the mandarins of the plain from the neighboring villages arrive, preceded by music and bringing me pastoral offerings, — baskets of preserved grapes, baskets of pears, live chickens in cages, and a jar of rice-wine. They wear the official winter head-dress, with a raven's quill, and have on gowns of dark silk with squares of gold embroidery, in the centre of which is depicted, surrounded by clouds, the invariable stork flying toward the moon. They are nearly all dried-up old men with gray beards and drooping gray moustaches. We have great *tchinchins* with them, profound bows, extravagant compliments, handshakings in which one feels the scratch of over-long nails, the touch of thin old fingers.

At two o'clock I remount with my men and start off through the dilapidated streets, preceded by the same procession as upon my arrival. The gongs are muffled, the heralds sound their cries. Behind me my host, the mandarin, follows in his palanquin, accompanied by the troop on stilts and by the enormous dragons.

As we leave the village, and enter the deep tunnelled gateway where the crowd is already assembled to see us, the whole procession is engulfed with us, — the long, striding princesses, the gods who play the cithern or the tambourine, the red beast, and the green beast. In the semi-obscurity of the arched way, to the noise of all the citherns and of all the gongs, in the clouds of black dust which blind us, there is a compact *mêlée*, where our horses prance and jump, troubled by the noise and terrified by the two frightful monsters undulating above our heads.

After conducting us a quarter of a league beyond the walls, the procession leaves us at last, and we find silence again on the burning plain, where we have about twenty kilometres to go through the dust and the "yellow wind" before reaching Y-Tchou, another old walled city which is to be our halting-place for the night.

Not until to-morrow do we arrive at the tombs.

III

The plain resembles that of yesterday, yet it is a little more green and wooded. The wheat, sown in rows, as with us, grows miraculously in this soil, made up of dust and cinders though it apparently is. Everything seems less desolate as one gets farther away from the region of Pekin, and ascends almost imperceptibly towards those great mountains of the west, which are appearing with greater and greater distinctness in front of us. The "yellow wind," too, blows with less severity, and when it dies down for a few moments, when the blinding dust decreases, it is like the country in the north of France, with its ploughed fields and clumps of elms and willows. One forgets that this is the heart of China, on the other side of the globe, and one expects to see peasants from home pass along the paths. But the few toilers who are bending over the earth have long braids, coiled about their heads like crowns, and their bare backs are saffron-colored.

All is peace in these sunshine-flooded fields, in these villages built in the scanty shade of the willows. The people seem to live happily, cultivating the friendly soil in primitive fashion, guided by the customs of five thousand years ago. Aside from the possible exactions of a few mandarins, — and there are many who are kind, — these Chinese peasants still live in the Golden Age, and I can hardly conceive of their accepting the joys of the "New China" dreamed of by Occidental reformers. Up to this time, it is true, the invasion has scarcely reached them; in this part of the country, occupied solely by the French, our troops have never played any other role than that of defender of the villagers against pillaging Boxers. Ploughing, sowing, all the work of the fields, has been quietly done in season, and it is impossible not to be struck with the very different look of other parts of the country which I will not designate, where there has been a reign of terror, and where the fields have been destroyed and have become desert steppes.

At about half-past four, against a background of mountains which are beginning to look tall to us, a village appears, the first sight of which, like that of yesterday, is rather formidable with its high crenellated ramparts.

A horseman comes out to meet me once more, like yesterday, and again it is the captain in command of the post of marine infantry stationed there since last autumn.

Watchers stationed on the walls have perceived us from afar by the cloud of dust our horses raise on the plain. As soon as we approach we see emerging from the old gates the official procession coming to meet us, with the same emblems as at Lai-

Chou-Chien, — the same big butterfly, the same red parasols, the same shields and banners. Each Chinese ceremonial has been for centuries regulated by unvarying usages.

However, the people who receive me to-day are much more elegant and undoubtedly richer than those of yesterday. The mandarin, who comes down from his sedan chair to await me at the side of the road, having sent his red paper visiting-card on before him a hundred feet or so, stands surrounded by a group of important-looking persons in sumptuous silk robes. He himself is a distinguished-looking old man, who wears in his hat the peacock feather and the sapphire button. There is an enormous crowd waiting to see me make my entrance to the funereal sound of the gongs and the prolonged cries of the heralds. On the top of the ramparts figures may be seen peering through the battlements with their small oblique eyes, and even in the dim gateways double rows of yellow men crowd against the walls. My interpreter confesses, however, that there is a general disappointment. "If he is a man of letters," they ask, "why is he dressed like a colonel?" (The scorn of the Chinese for the military profession is well known.) My horse, however, somewhat restores my prestige. Tired as the poor Algerian animal is, he still has a certain carriage of the head and tail when he feels that he is observed, and especially if he hears the sound of the gong.

Y-Tchou, the city wherein we find ourselves, shut in by walls thirty feet high, still contains fifteen thousand inhabitants in spite of its deserted districts and its ruins. There is a great crowd along our route, in all the little streets and in front of the little old shops where antediluvian occupations are carried on. It was from this very place that the terrible movement of hatred against foreigners was launched last year. In a convent of Bonze nuns in the neighboring mountain the war of extermination was first preached, and these people who receive me so kindly were the first Boxers. Ardent converts for the moment to the French cause, they cheerfully decapitate those of their own people who refuse to come to terms, and put their heads in the little cages which adorn the gates of their city; but if the wind should change to-morrow, I should see myself cut up by them to the tune of the same old gongs and with the same enthusiasm which they put into my reception. When I have taken possession of the house set apart for me, back of the residence of the mandarin at the end of an interminable avenue of old porticoes, and monsters who show me their teeth in tiger-like smiles, a half-hour of daylight still remains, and I go to pay a visit to a young prince of the imperial family, stationed at Y-Tchou in the interests of the venerable tombs.

First comes his garden, melancholy in the April twilight. It lies between walls of gray brick, and is very much shut in for a town already so walled. Gray also is the rockwork outlining the small squares or lozenges, where big red, lavender, and pink peonies flourish. These, unlike our own, are very fragrant, and to-night fill the air of this gloomy enclosure with an excessive odor. There are also rows of little porcelain jars inhabited by tiny fish — regular monstrosities — red fish or black fish with cumbersome fins and extravagant tails, giving the effect of a flounced petticoat; fish with enormous terrifying eyes, which protrude like those of the heraldic dragons and which are the result of I do not know what mysterious form of breeding. The Chinese, who torture the feet of their women, also deform their trees, so that they remain dwarfed and crooked. They train their fruits to resemble animals, and their animals to look like the chimæras of a dream.

It is already dark in the prince's apartment, which looks out on this prison-like garden, and one sees little, on first entering, but draperies of red silk, long canopies falling from numerous "parasols of honor," which are open and standing upright on wooden supports. The air is heavy, saturated with opium and musk. There are deep red divans with silver pipes lying about for smoking the poison of which China is in a fair way to perish. The prince, who is twenty or twenty-two years old, is of a sickly ugliness, with divergent eyes; he is perfumed to excess, and dressed in pale silk in tones of mauve or lilac.

In the evening dinner with the mandarin, where the commandant of the French post, the prince, two or three notables, and one of my "confrères," a member of the Academy of China, — a mandarin with a sapphire button, — are the guests. Seated in heavy square arm-chairs, there are six or seven of us around a table decorated with small, exquisite, and unusual bits of old porcelain, so tiny as to seem to be part of a doll service. Red candles in high copper chandeliers give us our light.

This very morning the entire province had orders to leave off the winter head-dress and to put on the summer one, — a conical affair, resembling a lamp-shade, from which fall tufts of reddish horse-hair or peacock's or crow's feathers, according to the rank of the wearer. And since it is the style to wear them at dinner, hats of this description make grotesque figures of the guests.

As for the ladies of the house, they, alas, remain invisible, and it would be the worst possible breach of good form to ask for them or to refer to them in any way. It is well known that a Chinaman compelled to speak of his wife must refer to her in an indirect way, using, whenever possible, a qualifying term, devoid of all compliment, as, for example, "my offensive" or "my nauseating" wife.

The dinner begins with preserved prunellas and a great variety of dainty sweetmeats, which are eaten with little chop-sticks. The mandarin makes excuses for not offering me sea-swallows' nests, but Y-Tchou is so far from the coast that it is difficult to secure what one would like. But to make up for this lack, there is a dish of sharks' fins, another of the bladder of the sperm whale, another still of hinds' nerves, besides a ragout of waterlily roots with shrimps' eggs.

The inevitable odor of opium and musk mingled with the flavor of strange sauces pervades the room, which is white with a black ceiling. Its walls are decorated with water-colors on long strips of precious yellow paper, containing representations of animals or of huge flowers. A score of servants flock about us with the same sort of head-dress as their masters, and clad in beautiful silk gowns with velvet corselets. At my right my "confrère" of the Chinese Academy discourses to me of another world. He is old and quite withered-looking from the abuse of the fatal drug; his small face, shrivelled to a mere nothing, is obliterated by his conical hat and by his big blue goggles.

"Is it true," he inquires, "that the Middle Empire occupies the top of the territorial globe, and that Europe hangs on one side at an uncomfortable angle?"

It appears that he has at the ends of his fingers more than forty thousand characters in writing, and that he is able to improvise sweet poetry on any subject you may choose. From time to time I am aghast at the sight of his skeleton-like arm emerging from sleeves like pagodas, and stretching out toward some dish. His object is to secure with his own two-tined fork some choice morsel for me, which compels me to resort to perpetual and difficult jugglery in order not to have to eat the things.

After several preposterous light dishes, boned ducks appear, then a copious variety of viands succeed one another until the guests announce that they really have had enough. Then they bring opium pipes and cigarettes, and soon it is time to take a palanquin for the nocturnal festival they are arranging for me.

Outside, in the long avenue of porticoes, under the starry sky, all the servants of the Yamen await us with big paper lanterns, painted with bats and chimæras. A hundred friendly Boxers are also there, holding torches to light us better. Each of us gets into a palanquin, and the bearers trot off with us, while flaming torches run along beside us, and gongs, also running, begin the noise of battle at the head of our procession.

By the light of dancing torches we file rapidly past the open stalls, past the groups of natives assembled to watch us, past the grimacing monsters ranged along our route.

At the rear of an immense court stands a new building, where by the light of the torches we read the astonishing inscription, "Parisiana of Y-Tchou." "Parisiana" in this ultra-Chinese town, which until the previous autumn had never seen a European approach its walls! Our bearers stop there, and we find it is a theatre improvised this winter by our sixty soldiers to help pass away the glacial evenings.

I had promised to assist at a gala performance given for me by these grown-up children this evening. And of all the charming receptions that have been tendered me here and there all over the world, none has moved me more than this one arranged by a few soldiers exiled in a lost corner of China. Their reserved smiles of welcome, the few words one of them undertook to say for all, were more touching than any banquet or formal address, and I was glad to press the hands of the brave soldiers who dared not offer them.

In order that I might have a souvenir of their evening's hospitality at Y-Tchou, they got up a subscription and presented me with a very local gift, — one of those red silk parasols with long falling draperies, which it is the custom in China to carry in front of men of mark. And cumbrous as the thing is, even when folded, it is needless to say that I shall take it with great care to France.

They next gave me an illustrated programme, on which the name of each actor figured, followed by a pompous title, — "Monsieur the soldier so-and-so of the Comédie-Française," or "Monsieur the corporal so-and-so of the Théâtre Sarah-Bernhardt." We take our places. It is a real theatre that they have made, with a raised stage, scenery, and a curtain.

In the Chinese arm-chairs, which are placed in the first row, their captain is seated next to me; then come the mandarin, the prince of the blood, and two or three other notables, with long queues. Behind us are the under-officers and the soldiers; several yellow babies in ceremonial toilettes mingle familiarly with them, even climbing up on their knees. They are pupils from their school. For they have started a school, like the one at Lai-Chou-Chien, to teach French to the children of the neighborhood. A sergeant presented me to an inimitable youngster of not more than six, dressed for the occasion in a beautiful gown, his little short, thick queue tied with red silk, who recited for me the beginning of "Maître corbeau sur un arbre perché," in a deep voice, rolling his eyes to the ceiling the while.

Three taps and the curtain rises. First comes a farce, by I know not whom, but certainly much retouched by themselves with an unexpected turn of wit which is irresistible. The ladies, the mothers-in-law, with false hair made of oakum, are indescribable. Then more comic scenes and songs from the "Black Cat." The Chinese guests on their throne-like chairs remain as impassive as the Buddhas of the pagodas. What do their Asiatic brains make of all this French gaiety?

Before the last numbers on the programme are over the sudden thundering of gongs is heard outside, the playing of citherns, and the clashing of cymbals, and of all the rest of the iron instruments of China. It is the prelude to the fête which the mandarin is to give me, which is to take place in the courtyard of the army quarters, and in which our soldiers naturally are to take part.

A profusion of lanterns illumines the court, together with the flaming torches of a hundred Boxers. First there is a stilt dance, then follow all the gymnastic societies of the adjoining district in their specialties. Little country boys twelve years old, costumed like lords of old dynasties, have a sham battle, flourishing their swords and jumping about like kittens, prodigies of quickness and lightness. Then come the young men of another village, who throw off their garments and begin to twirl pitchforks all around their naked bodies; by a twist of the wrist or by an imperceptible movement of the foot they are turned so rapidly that very soon they are no longer forks to our eyes, but a row of endless serpents about the breasts of the men. Then suddenly, more deftly than in the best managed circus, a horizontal bar is placed before us, and acrobats, naked to the waist, and superbly muscular, give a performance. They belong to the mandarin, and are the very men who just now served us at the table in beautiful silken robes.

It all ended with very long and noisy fireworks. When the pieces attached to invisible bamboo stems exploded in the air, delicate and luminous paper pagodas floated off across the starry sky, fabrics of a Chinese dream, trembling, imponderable, which suddenly took fire and disappeared in smoke.

It is late when we return through the little dark streets, now all asleep. Our bearers trot along, escorted by a thousand dancing lights from torches and lanterns.

Toward midnight I am at last alone, in the depths of the Yamen, in my separate dwelling, the avenue leading to it guarded by motionless, crouching beasts. On my centre-table they have placed a luncheon of all the kinds of cakes known to China. Trees in fruit, in flower, and without leaves, decorate my small tables, — dwarf trees, of course, grown in porcelain jars, and so tortured as to become unnatural. A little pear-tree has assumed the regular form of a lyre composed of white blossoms; a small peach-tree resembles a crown made of pink flowers. Everything in my room, except these fresh spring plants, is old, warped, worm-eaten, and at the holes in a ceiling that was once white appear the faces of innumerable rats, whose eyes follow me about the room. As soon as I put out my light and lie down in my great bed with carvings representing horrible animals, I hear all these rats come down, move about among the fine porcelains, and gnaw at my cakes. Then from out the more and more profound stillness of my surroundings the night watchmen with muffled steps begin discreetly to use their castanets.

SUNDAY, April 28.

An early morning walk among the silver-sculptors of Y-Tchou, then through a quite dead part of the town to an antique pagoda half crumbled away, which stands among some phantom trees of which little but the bark is left. Along its galleries the tortures of the Buddhist hell are depicted; several hundred life-sized persons carved in wood filled with worm-holes, are fighting with devils who are tearing them to pieces or burning them alive.

At nine o'clock I mount my horse and start off with my men, in order to cover before noon the fifteen or eighteen kilometres which still separate me from the mysterious burial-places of the emperors; for we return to Y-Tchou for the night, and set off again to-morrow on the road to Pekin.

We go out at the gate opposite the one we entered yesterday. Nowhere else have we seen so many monsters as in this ancient town; their great sneering faces appear on all sides out of the ground, where time has almost buried them. A few entire figures may be seen crouching on their pedestals, guarding the approaches to the granite bridges or ranged in rows around the squares.

As we leave the town, we pass a poor-looking pagoda on whose walls hang cages containing human heads recently cut off. And then we find ourselves once more in the silent fields under the burning sun.

The prince accompanies us, riding a Mongolian colt as rough-coated as a spaniel. His rose-colored silks and velvet foot-gear form a striking contrast to our rough costumes and dusty boots, and he leaves behind him a trail of musk.

IV

The country slopes gently toward the range of Mongolian mountains, which, though still some distance ahead of us, is now growing rapidly in height. Trees are more and more frequent, grass grows naturally here and there, and we have left the dreary ashy soil.

Near by there are a few pointed-topped hills, queerly shaped, with occasionally an old tower perched on the summit, — the ten or twelve storied kind, which at once give the landscape a Chinese look, with superimposed roofs, curved up like dogs' ears, at the corners, with an Æolian harp at each end.

The air is growing purer; the cloud of dust is left behind as we approach the unquestionably privileged region which has been selected for the repose of the celestial emperors and empresses.

We stop at a village, after about a dozen kilometres, to take breakfast with a great prince of much higher rank than the one who rides with us. He is a direct uncle of the Emperor, in disgrace with the Empress, whose favorite he has been, and now entrusted with the guardianship of the tombs. As he is in deep mourning, he is dressed in cotton like the poor, and yet does not resemble them. He makes excuses for receiving us in a dilapidated old house, his own Yamen having been burned by the Germans, and offers us a very Chinese breakfast, where reappear the sharks' wings and hinds' nerves. The flat-faced peasants of the neighborhood peer at us in the meantime through the numerous holes in the rice-paper window-panes.

We remount at once, after the last cup of tea, to visit the tombs toward which we have been journeying for three days, and which are now very near. My confrère of the Pekin Academy, with his big, round spectacles and his little bird-like body completely lost in his beautiful silken robes, has rejoined us, and slowly follows along upon a mule.

A more and more solitary country. No more villages, no more fields! The road winds along among the hills, — which are covered with grass and flowers, — surprising and enchanting our unaccustomed eyes. It seems like a glimpse of Eden after the dusty-gray China we have come through, where the only green thing was the wheat. The perpetual dust of Petchili has been left behind; but on the plain below we still perceive it, like a fog from which we have escaped.

We continue to mount, and soon arrive at the first spurs of the Mongolian range. Here behind a wall of earth we find an immense Tartar camp, at least two thousand men, armed with lances, bows, and arrows, guard of honor of the defunct rulers.

Once more we see a clear horizon, the very memory of which had faded. It seems as though these Mongolian mountains suddenly huddled together as though they had all pressed forward; very rocky they are, with strange outlines, peaks like turrets or pagoda-towers rising above us, — all of a beautiful purple iris effect.

Ahead of us we begin to see on all sides wooded valleys and forests of cedar. True, they are artificial forests, although very old, — planted centuries ago for this funeral park, covering an area twenty miles in circumference, where four Tartar emperors sleep.

We enter this silent, shadowy place, astonished to find that, contrary to Chinese custom, it is surrounded by no wall. No doubt it was felt that this isolated spot would be sufficiently protected by the terror inspired by the shades of the emperors, as well as by a general edict of death promulgated in advance against any one who dared to cultivate a bit of the ground or even sow a seed.

It is the sacred wood *par excellence*, with all its retirement and its mystery. What marvellous poets of the dead the Chinese are, to be able to prepare them such dwelling-places!

Here in the shadows one is tempted to speak low, as under the roof of a temple; one feels it a profanity for the horses to trample down the turf, — a carpet of fine grass and blossoms, venerated for ages past, and apparently never disturbed. The great cedars and the hundred-year-old thuyas, scattered over the hills and in the valleys, are separated by open spaces where brushwood grows; and under the colonnade formed by their massive trunks there is nothing but short grass, exquisite tiny flowers, and moss and lichens.

The dust that obscures the sky on the plains apparently never reaches this chosen spot, for the magnificent green of the trees is nowhere dimmed. In this superb solitude, which men have created here and dedicated to the shades of their masters, the distance disclosed to us as our road takes us past some clearing or up some height is of an absolute limpidity. A light as from Paradise falls upon us from a heaven profoundly blue, streaked with tiny clouds, rose-gray like turtle-doves. At such moments one gets a glimpse of splendid distant golden-yellow roofs rising amongst sombre branches, like the palace of the Sleeping Beauty.

Not a soul in all this shaded road. The silence of the desert! Only occasionally the croaking of a raven, — too funereal a bird, it seems, for the calm enchantment of this place, where Death is compelled, before entering, to lay aside its horror and to become simply the magician of unending rest.

In some places the trees form avenues which are finally lost to sight in the green dusk. Elsewhere they have been planted without design, and seem to have grown of their own accord and to form a natural forest. All the details recall the fact that the place is magnificent, imperial, sacred; the smallest bridge, thrown over a stream which crosses the road, is of white marble of rare design, covered with beautiful carvings; an heraldic beast, crouching in the shadow, menaces us with a ferocious smile as we pass by, or a marble obelisk surrounded by five-clawed dragons rises unexpectedly in its snowy whiteness, outlined against the dark background of the cedars.

In this wood, twenty miles in circumference, lie the bodies of but four emperors; that of the Empress Regent, whose tomb was long since begun, will be added as well as her son's, the young Emperor, who has had his chosen place marked with a stele of gray marble[4]. And that is all. Other sovereigns, past or to be, sleep, or will sleep, elsewhere, in other Edens, as vast and as wonderfully arranged. Immense space is required for the body of a Son of Heaven, and immense solitary silence must reign round about it.

The arrangement of these tombs is regulated by unchangeable plans, which date back to old extinguished dynasties. They are all alike, recalling those of the Ming emperors, which antedate them by several centuries, and whose ruins have been for a long time the object of one of the excursions permitted to European travellers.

One invariably approaches by a cut in the sombre forest, half

---

4 His subjects have had engraven on this stele an inscription expressing the hope that their sovereign may live ten times ten thousand years.

a mile in length, which has been so planned by the artists of the past that it opens, like the doors of a magnificent stage-setting, upon some incomparable background such as a particularly high mountain, abrupt and bold, or a mass of rock presenting one of those anomalies of form and color that the Chinese everywhere seek.

Invariably, also, the avenue begins with great triumphal arches of white marble, which are, needless to say, surmounted by monsters bristling with horns and claws.

In the case of the ancestor of the present Emperor, who receives to-day our first visit, these entrance arches appear unexpectedly in the heart of the forest, their bases entangled with wild bindweed. They seem to have shot up, at the rubbing of an enchanter's magic ring, out of what appears to be virgin soil, so covered is it with moss and with the rare delicate little plants which nothing disturbs, and which grow only in places that have long been quiet and respected by man.

Next come some marble bridges with semicircular arches; there are three bridges exactly alike, for each time an emperor passes, dead or alive, the middle bridge is reserved for him alone. The architects of the tombs were careful to have the avenue crossed several times by artificial streams, in order to have an occasion for spanning them with these charming curves of everlasting white. On each rail of the bridge there is an intertwining of imperial fancies. The sloping pavement is white and slippery, and completely framed in grass, which pushes through and flourishes in all its joinings.

The crossing is dangerously slippery for our horses, whose steps resound mournfully on the marble; the sudden noise we make in the stillness is almost a source of embarrassment to us, making us feel as though our coming had disturbed in an unseemly manner the composure of the necropolis. With the exception of ourselves and a few ravens in the trees, nothing moves and nothing lives in all the immensity of this memorial park.

Beyond the three arched bridges the avenue leads to the first temple, with a yellow enamelled roof, which seems to bar our way. At the four corners of the open space it occupies, rise four rostral columns made of marble, white as ivory, — admirable monoliths, with a crouching animal at the top of each one, similar to those enthroned on the obelisks in front of the palace at Pekin, — a sort of slender jackal, with long, erect ears, upturned eyes, and a mouth open as if howling to heaven. This first temple contains nothing but three giant stele, resting on marble turtles as large as leviathans. They recount the glory of a defunct emperor; the first is inscribed in the Tartar language, the second in Chinese, the third in Manchou.

Beyond this temple of stele the avenue is prolonged in the same direction for an indefinite length, very majestic with its two walls of blackgreen cedars, and its carpet of grass, flowers, and moss, which looks as though it were never trampled upon. All the avenues in these woods are always thus deserted, always silent, for the Chinese come here only at rare intervals, in solemn, respectful processions to perform their funeral rites. And it is the air of desertion in the midst of splendor which is the great charm of this place, unique in all the world.

When the Allies have left China, this park of tombs, open to us for a single moment, will be once more impenetrable for how long we do not know; perhaps until another invasion, which may cause the venerable yellow Colossus to crumble away, — unless, indeed, it awakes from its slumber of a thousand years; for the Colossus is still capable of spreading terror, and of arming itself for a revenge of which one dares not think — *Mon Dieu!* the day when China, in the place of its small regiments of mercenaries and bandits, shall arm in mass for a supreme revolt its millions of young peasants such as I have recently seen, sober, cruel, spare, muscular, accustomed to every sort of physical exercise, and defiant of death, what a terrifying army it will have, if modern instruments of destruction are placed in their hands! On reflection, it seems as though certain of the Allies have been rather rash to have sown here so many seeds of hatred, and to have created so much desire for vengeance.

Now, at the end of the dark deserted green avenue the final temple shows its shining roof. The mountain above, the strange, crenellated mountain, which has been chosen as a sort of background for all this sad creation, rises to-day all violet and rose against a bit of rare blue sky, — the blue of a turquoise turning to green. The light continues to be modified, exquisite; the sun is veiled by the same clouds that in color remind one of turtle-doves, and we no longer hear our horses' steps, so thick is the carpet of grass and moss.

Now one catches sight of the great triple doors of the sanctuary; they are blood-red with hinges of gold. Then comes the whiteness of three marble bridges with slippery pavements, in crossing which my little army makes an exaggerated noise, as though the rows of cedars ranged like a wall on either side of us had the sonority of a church. From here on, as if to guard the ever more sacred approach, tall marble statues are lined up on each side of the avenue. We pass between motionless elephants, horses, lions, and mute white warriors, three times the height of man.

As we approach the white terraces of the temple we begin to perceive the ravages of war. The German soldiers, who were here before ours, tore out in places, with the points of their swords, the beautiful gilded bronze decorations of the red doors, taking them to be gold.

In the first court of one of the lateral edifices, whose roofs are as sumptuously enamelled as those of the big sanctuary, are the kitchens, — where are prepared at certain times repasts for the Shadow of Death, — extensive enough to provide for a legion of ogres or vampires. Enormous ovens, enormous bronze troughs in which whole oxen are cooked, are still intact; but the pavement is littered with broken porcelains, with fragments which are the result of a blow with the butt end of a gun or a bayonet.

On a high terrace, after passing two or three courts paved with marble, after two or three enclosures entered by triple doors of cedar, the central temple opens before us, empty and devastated. It is magnificent in its proportions, with tall columns of red and gold lacquer, but it has been despoiled of its sacred riches. Heavy silk hangings, idols, silver drinking-vessels, flat silver dishes for the feasts of the Shades had almost entirely disappeared when the French arrived, and what remained of the treasures has been collected in a safe place by our officers. Two of them have just been decorated by the Emperor of China for this preservation of property, and it is one of the most curious episodes of this abnormal war, the sovereign of the invaded country spontaneously decorating the officers of the invading army out of gratitude. Behind the last temple is the colossal tomb.

For the interment of an emperor the Chinese cut a piece out of a hill as one would cut out a portion from a Titanic cake; then they isolate it by enormous excavations and surround it with crenellated ramparts. It thus becomes a massive citadel. Then in the bowels of the earth they dig a sepulchral passageway known only to the initiated, and at its end they place the emperor, not mummified, but in a thick coffin made of cedar lacquered in gold, which must prevent rapid disintegration. Then they seal forever the subterranean door by a kind of screen of faience, invariably yellow and green, with relief representing the lotus, dragons, or clouds. Each sovereign in his turn is buried and sealed up in the same manner, — in the midst of a forest region equally vast and equally solitary.

At last we arrive at the end of this section of a hill and of this rampart, stopped in our course by a melancholy screen of yellow and green faience, which seems to be the end of our forty-league journey. It is a square screen, twenty feet each way, brilliant with color and varnish, and in striking contrast to the gray brick wall and gray earth.

The ravens are massed here as though they divined the sinister thing concealed from them in the heart of the mountain, and receive us with a chorus of cries.

Opposite the faience screen is an altar of roughhewn marble, whose brutal simplicity is in striking contrast to the splendors of the temple and the avenue. It supports a sort of incense burner of unknown and tragic significance, and two or three symbolic articles intentionally rude in workmanship. One is confounded by the strange forms, the almost primitive barbarity of these last and supreme objects at the threshold of the tomb; their aspect is intended to create a sort of indefinable terror. I remember once, in the holy mountain at Nikko, where sleep the emperors of old Japan, that after the fairy-like magnificence of gold-lacquered temples, outside the little bronze door which forms the entrance to each sepulture, I stumbled against just such an altar, supporting two or three worn emblems, as disturbing as these in their artificial barbaric *naïveté*.

It seems that in these subterranean passages of the Son of Heaven there are heaps of treasures, precious stones, and metals. Those who are authorities in Chinese matters assured our generals that enough would be found about the body of a single emperor to pay the war indemnity demanded by Europe, and that the mere threat of violating one of these ancestral tombs would suffice to bring the Regent and her son to Pekin submissive and yielding, ready to make all concessions.

Happily for our Occidental honor, no one of the Allies would consent to this means, so the yellow and green faience screens have not been broken; every dragon, every lotus, no matter how delicate in relief, has remained intact. All have paused here. The old emperors, behind their everlasting walls, may have heard the approach of the trumpets of the barbarian army and the beating of their drums, but each one of them could fall asleep again, tranquil as before, surrounded by the empty glory of his fabulous wealth.

Chapter VIII

The Last Days of Pekin

I

PEKIN, Wednesday May 1.

I RETURNED YESTERDAY from my visit to the tombs of the emperors after three days and a half of journeying in the haze created by the "yellow wind," beneath a heavy sun constantly obscured by the dust. I am back once more in Pekin, with our chief general, in my old rooms in the Palace of the North. Yesterday the thermometer registered 40° in the shade, to-day only 8° (a difference of 32° in twenty-four hours). An icy wind drives the rain-drops that are mingled with a few white flakes, and the neighboring mountains behind the Summer Palace are quite covered with snow. Yet there are people in France who complain of our springs!

Now that my expedition is over, I ought at once to go back to Taku and the squadron, but the general wants me to stay for a great fête he is to give to the staff officers of the allied armies, and so I have telegraphed to the admiral, asking for three days more.

In the evening I walk on the esplanade of the Rotunda Palace in company with Colonel Marchand. The weather is bad, stormy, and cold, and the twilight comes on too early on account of the rapidly moving clouds. As the wind parts them one gets glimpses of the mountains behind the Summer Palace, snowy white against a background of dark clouds.

Confusion reigns about us, but it is the confusion of a fête

instead of that incidental to battle and death, as I had known it here last autumn. Zouaves and African chasseurs are running about, carrying ladders, draperies, and armfuls of branches and flowers. The old cedars in the vicinity of the beautiful pagoda shining with enamel, lacquer, and gold, are disguised until they look like fruit-trees; upon their almost sacred branches are thousands of yellow balls that look like big oranges. Chains supporting garlands of Chinese lanterns go from one to the other.

It is Colonel Marchand who has planned it all. "Do you think it will be pretty? Do you think it will be a little unusual? You see, I want to do it better than the others."

The others were the Germans, the Americans, and all the rest of the Allies who have given these fêtes before the French. So my new friend has been in the most feverish state of activity for five or six days, in attempting to do something that has never been done before, working far into the night with his men, who share his enthusiasm, putting into this play-work the same passionate effort he put into conducting his little army across Africa. From time to time, though, his smile betrays that he is finding amusement in all this, and will not take its possible failure tragically, if wind and snow come to upset the fairyland of his dreams.

No, but this cold is annoying all the same! What shall we do, since it is to take place in the open air on the terraces of the palace, if the north wind should blow? What of the illuminations, of the awnings? And the women, won't they freeze in their evening gowns? For there are women even here in the heart of the Yellow City.

Suddenly a gust of wind breaks down a whole string of lanterns with pearl pendants, which are already hung from the branches of the old cedars, and upsets a row of the flower-pots, which have been brought up here by the hundreds to give life to these old gardens.

THURSDAY, May 2.

Messengers have been sent to the four corners of Pekin, announcing that this evening's fête has been postponed until Saturday, in the hope that the bad weather will be over by that time. So I have had to send a despatch, asking the admiral for a prolongation of my freedom. I came away for three days and have remained almost a month, and am wearing shirts and waistcoats borrowed here and there from my various army friends.

This morning I have the honor of breakfasting with our neighbor in the Yellow City, Marshal von Waldersee.

Covers are laid for the marshal and his staff in a large room finished in marquetry and carvings, in a part of the palace untouched by the flames. They are all correctly attired in irreproachable military garb in the midst of this fantastically Chinese setting.

It is the first time in my life that I have sat down at a table with German officers, and I had not anticipated the pang of anguish with which I arrived among them as a guest. Oh, the memories of thirty years ago, and the special aspects which that terrible year had for me!

That long winter of 1870 was passed in a wretched little boat on the coast of Prussia. How well I remember my watch on the cold decks, — child that I was, almost, — and the silhouette of a certain *King William* that so often appeared on the horizon in pursuit of us, at the sight of which we always fled, its balls whizzing behind us over the icy waters. Then the despair of feeling that our small part there had been so useless and unavailing! We knew nothing about it until long afterward; news came seldom, and when it did come it was in little sealed papers that we opened tremblingly. Over each fresh disaster, over each

new story of German cruelty, what rage filled our hearts, —
childlike in the excess of their violence, — what vows we made
among ourselves never to forget! All this came to me pell-mell,
or rather a rapid synthesis of it all, on the very threshold of this
breakfast-room, even before I had crossed the sill, from the mere
sight of the pointed helmets that hung along the wall, and I felt
like going away.

But I did not, and the feeling disappeared in the dark backward
and abysm of time. Their welcome, their handshakes, and their
smiles of good fellowship made me forget it in a second, for the
moment at least. At any rate, it seems that there is not between
them and us that racial antipathy which is less easily overcome
than the sharp rancor of war.

During breakfast this Chinese palace of theirs, accustomed
to the sound of gongs and flutes, echoes to the strains of
"Lohengrin" or the "Rheingold," played in the distance by their
military band. The white-haired marshal was good enough to
give me a seat near him, and, like all of our people who have
had the honor to come under his influence, I felt the charm of his
exquisite distinction of manner, of his kindness and goodness.

FRIDAY, May 3.

More and more people are coming back to Pekin, until it is almost
as crowded as of yore. The people are very much occupied with
funerals. Last summer the Chinese here were killing one another;
now they are burying one another. Every family has kept its dead
in the house for months, according to their custom, in thick cedar
coffins, which somewhat modify the odor of decay; they bring
the dead their daily meals as well as presents; they burn red
wax candles for them; they give them music; they play the flute
and the gong in the continual fear of not paying them enough
honor and of incurring their vengeance and their ill will. The

time has come now to take them to their graves, with processions a kilometre long, with more flutes and gongs, innumerable lanterns and gilded emblems, which they hire at high prices; they ruin themselves for monuments and offerings; they scarcely sleep for fear of seeing their dead return. I do not remember who it was who described China as "a country where a few hundred millions of living Chinese are dominated and terrorized by a few thousand millions of dead ones." Tombs everywhere and of every form; one sees nothing else on the plains of Pekin. As for all the thickets of cedar, pine, and arbor-vitæ, they are nothing but funeral parks, walled in by double or triple walls, a single park often being consecrated to one person, thus cutting the living off from an enormous amount of space.

A defunct Lama, whom I visited to-day, occupies on his own account a space two or three kilometres square. The old trees in his park, scarcely leafed out as yet, give little shade from the sun, which is already dangerously hot. In the centre of it is a marble mausoleum, — a pyramidal structure with small figures and masses of white carvings which taper skyward, terminating in gilt tips. Scattered about under the cedars are crumbling old temples, built long ago to the memory of this holy man, enclosing in their obscurity a whole population of gilded idols that are turning to dust. Just outside, the cindery soil where no one ever walks, is strewn with the resinous cones from the trees, and with the black feathers of the crows, who inhabit this silent place by the hundreds. As in the imperial woods, April has brought out a few violet gillyflowers and a quantity of very small iris of the same color.

All the woods which are used for burial places — and the country is encumbered with them — resemble this one, and contain the same old temples, the same idols, and the same crows.

The plains of Petchili are an immense necropolis, where the living tremble lest they offend one of the innumerable dead.

Pekin is not only being repeopled, but rebuilt; hastily though, out of small blackened bricks from the ruins, so that the new streets will probably never display the luxurious façades, the lacy, gilded wood-work of former times.

The great eastern artery that crosses the Tartar City is, of all the streets of old Pekin, the nearest to what it used to be; life here is becoming intense, the people swarm. For the length of a league this avenue, which is fifty metres wide, — of magnificent proportions, although now very much injured, — is invaded by thousands of platforms, sheds, tents, or in some cases simply umbrellas stuck in the ground, where the people who serve horrible drinks and food dispense their wares, always in delicate China very much decorated; there are charlatans, acupuncturers, Punch-and-Judy shows, musicians, and story-tellers. The crowd is divided into an infinite number of currents by all these small shops and theatres, like the waters of a river filled with islands, so that there is a constant eddy of human heads black with dust and filth. Rough, hoarse vociferations, in a quality of voice unfamiliar to our ears, are heard on all sides, to an accompaniment of grating violins, noisy gongs and bells. The caravans of enormous Mongolian camels, which all winter encumber the streets in endless processions, have disappeared in the solitudes of the North, together with their flat-faced drivers, who wish to escape the torrid heat; but their place in the central part of the street, reserved for animals and vehicles, is taken by numerous small horses and tiny carriages, and the cracking of whips is heard on all sides.

On the ground in front of the houses, spread out upon the mud and filth, the extravagant rag-fair that began last autumn is still going on; the remains of so much pillage and burning are left that it seems as though there was no end to them, — magnificently embroidered clothing spotted with blood, Buddhas, grotesque figures, jewels, dead men's wigs, cracked vases, or precious fragments of jade.

Behind all these ridiculous things, behind all this dusty display, the greater number of the houses, in contrast with the poverty-stricken appearance of the crowds, seem astonishingly rich in carvings and decorations, — a mass of openwork and fine gilding from top to bottom. Indefatigable artists, with the Chinese patience and skill which confound us, have carved crowds of little figures, monsters, and birds in the midst of flowers, and trees on which you can count the leaves.

Last summer, while the Boxers were burning so continually, these astonishing façades, representing an incalculable amount of human labor, were consumed by the hundreds; they made Pekin a veritable museum of carving and gold, the like of which men of to-day will never again have the time to construct.

SATURDAY, May 4.

The fête given by our general to the staff officers of the Allies is really coming off to-night. But before this we are to have a celebration among ourselves: the inauguration of a new boulevard in our quarter, from the Marble Bridge to the Yellow Gate, — a long boulevard whose construction was entrusted to Colonel Marchand, and which is to bear the name of our general. Never since the far-distant epoch when her network of paved avenues was laid out has Pekin seen such a thing, — a straight, level roadway, without ruts or humps, where carriages may drive rapidly between two rows of young trees.

There is a great crowd to assist at this inauguration. On both sides of the new, freshly gravelled, and still empty avenue — barred off by sentinels and ropes from one end to the other — all our soldiers are lined up, with a sprinkling of German soldiers too, for they are quite neighborly with ours, and a few Chinese, both men and women, in festive array. Quaint, charming babies, with cat-like eyes that slant upward toward the temple, occupy the first row, directly behind the rope; our soldiers are carrying some of them so that they may see better, and one big Zouave is walking up and down with two Chinese children, three or four years old, one on each shoulder. There are people on the roofs, too, — many of the convalescents are standing about on the tiled roof of our hospital, and some African chasseurs, seeking a choice place, have climbed the Gothic tower of the church, which, with the big tricolored flag floating in the breeze, dominates the entire scene.

There are French flags over all the Chinese doors, and they are arranged in groups, like trophies, with lanterns and garlands on all the poles. It is like a sort of foreign exotic Fourteenth of July; if it were in France the decorations would be commonplace; but here, in Pekin, they are touching and fine, especially when the military band arrives, and the "Marseillaise" bursts forth.

The inauguration consists simply of a sort of charge, executed on the fresh gravel by all the French officers, from the Yellow Gate to the other extremity of the boulevard, where the general awaits them on a balcony trimmed with garlands of green, and smilingly offers them champagne. Then the frail barriers are removed, the crowd disperses gaily, the children with the cat-like eyes trudge off over the well-rolled avenue, and all is over.

When we have all returned to France, and Pekin is again in the hands of the Chinese, I fear that this Avenue du Général-Vayron — though they now appear to appreciate it — will not last two winters.

II

EIGHT O'CLOCK IN the evening. The long May twilight is almost over, and the curious lanterns, some of glass with long strings of pearls, others of rice-paper in the form of birds or of lotus blossoms, are everywhere lighted among the old cedar branches on the esplanade of the Rotunda Palace, which I had known plunged in such a melancholy abyss of sadness and silence. To-night all is movement, life, gay light. Already uniformed officers of all the nations of Europe, and Chinese, in long silken robes, with official head-dresses from which depend peacock feathers, are going and coming amid the wonderful decorations. A table for seventy is set under a tent, and we are awaiting our incongruous assembly of guests.

Followed by small suites, they arrive from all quarters of Pekin, some on horseback, others in carriages, in chairs, or in sumptuous palanquins. As soon as any person of distinction appears at the lower door of the inclined plane, one of our military band, who is on the lookout, orders the playing of the national air of his country. The Russian Hymn follows the German, or the Japanese the march of the Bersaglieri. Even the Chinese air is heard, for some one pompously enters with a large red paper, which proves to be the visiting-card of Li-Hung-Chang, who is below, but who, in accordance with the etiquette of his country, is announced before he makes his appearance. Preceded by similar cards, the Chief-Justice of Pekin and the Representative Extraordinary of the Empress are the next to arrive. These Chinese princes, who are to assist at our fête, come in gala palanquins, with a cavalry escort, and they make their entrance with the most inscrutable expressions on their faces, followed by a band of servants dressed in silk. It was hard to have them! But Colonel Marchand, with the general's permission, made it a point of honor to invite them. Mixed in with our Western uniforms, mandarins' robes and pointed hats with the coral button are numerous. Their presence at this barbarian feast right in the heart of the Imperial City, which we have profaned, will remain one of the most singular inconsistencies of our time.

Such a length of table as there is, — its legs resting on an imperial carpet which seems to be made of thick yellow velvet! Bunches of flowers are arranged in priceless, gigantic old cloisonné vases that have been taken out of the reserves of the Empress for a single night. Marshal von Waldersee, with the wife of the French minister at his side, occupies the seat of honor; then two bishops in violet robes, the generals and officers of the seven allied nations, five or six women in evening dress, and, lastly, the three great princes of China, so enigmatical in their embroidered silks, their eyes partly concealed by their ceremonial hats and falling plumes.

At the close of this strange dinner, when the roses in the big, precious vases are beginning to hang their heads, our general, toward the close of his toast, turns to the Yellow Princes: "Your presence here among us," he says, "is a sufficient proof that we did not come here to make war against China, but only against an abominable sect," etc.

Then the Empress's representative takes up the ball with a suppleness characteristic of the far East, and, without turning a hair, replies (he was secretly a furious Boxer): "In the name of Her Imperial Chinese Majesty, I thank the generous nations of Europe for having extended a helping hand to our government in one of the gravest crises it has ever passed through."

A stupefied silence follows, and then glasses are emptied.

During the banquet the esplanade is filled with many uniformed and gaily dressed persons, of all sorts and colors, who are invited for the evening. The toasts having come to an end with the reply of the Chinese, I lean over the edge of the terrace to watch from on high and from afar the lighting up of the entire place below.

Coming out from under the awnings and the cedar branches, which obscure the view, it is a surprise and a delight to see the borders of the lake and the melancholy, silent landscape, — in ordinary times dark, disturbing, ghostly places as soon as night approaches, — as the lights come on as if for some fantastic apotheosis.

Soldiers have been stationed in all the old palaces and temples that are scattered amongst the trees, and in less than an hour, by climbing along the enamelled tiles, they have lighted innumerable red lanterns, which form lines of fire, outlining the curves of the multiple-storied roofs and emphasizing the Chinese characteristic of the architecture and the eccentricity of the miradors and towers. All along the tragic lake where the bodies still lie, concealed in the grass, is a row of lights; and as far as one can see the entire shadowy park, so ruined and desolate, creates an illusion of gaiety. The old dungeon on the Island of Jade throws out bright rays and blue fire. The Empress's gondolas, so long stationary, and more or less damaged, are out to-night on the reflecting waters, which, with the lights, remind one of Venice. For a single night an appearance of life pervades these phantoms of real things. And all this, never seen before, will never be seen again.

What an astounding contrast with what I used to see when I was alone in this palace in the autumn twilight! Along the lake groups of people in ball dress instead of corpses, — my only neighbors last year, — and the soft mildness of this May night instead of the glacial cold with which I used to shiver as soon as the sun began to go down.

In the foreground, at the entrance to the Marble Bridge, the great Arc de Triomphe of China, resplendent with gilding, shines out against the evening sky, its values all emphasized by a profusion of lights. Then the bridge across the lake is much lighted, although it seems luminous itself in its eternal whiteness. In the distance the whole phantasmagoria — empty palaces and pagodas — emerges from the obscurity of the trees, and is reflected in the water in lines of fire.

Our five hundred guests are scattered about in sympathetic groups on the borders of the lake beneath the spring-like verdure of the willows, along the Marble Bridge or in the imperial gondolas. As they come down from the terrace they are given gaily decorated lanterns on little sticks, so that after a time these balls of color, scattered along the paths, seem from a distance like a company of glow-worms.

From where I stand women in light evening wraps may be seen on the arms of officers, crossing the white paving-stones of the bridge, or seated in the stern of the long imperial barques, softly propelled by the oarsmen. How strange it seems to see these Europeans, almost all of whom underwent the tortures of the siege, walking quietly about in dinner dress in the retreat of the sovereigns who had secretly conspired to kill them!

Decidedly the place has lost all its horrors; there is so much light, so many people, so many soldiers, that all the vague forms of ghosts and evil spirits have been driven away for the night.

Something like approaching thunder is heard in the distance, which proves to be the noise of about fifty tambourines announcing the arrival of the procession. It was to form at the Yellow Gate, so as to follow the line of the new avenue, and to disband at the foot of the Rotunda Palace. The lights of the first division appear at the entrance of the Marble Bridge, and begin to cross its magnificent white archway. Cavalry, infantry, and music, all seem to be rolling on in our direction, with enough noise from the brasses and the tambourines to make the sepulchral walls of the Violet City tremble, while above the heads of the thousands of soldiers groups and rows of extravagantly Chinese colored lanterns are swinging to the movement of the horses' hoofs or to the rhythm of human shoulders.

The troops have passed, but the procession is not nearly over. A sharp, delirious noise that gets on one's nerves follows the marches played by our musicians, — the noise of gongs, zithers, cymbals, bells. At the same time gigantic green and yellow banners, curiously slashed and of unusual proportions, begin to appear on the Marble Bridge, borne by an advancing company of tall, slender persons, with astonishing underpinnings, who are swinging along like bears. They prove to be my stilt walkers from Y-Tchou and from Lai-Chou-Chien from the vicinity of the tombs, who have taken a three or four days' journey in order to participate in this French fête!

Behind them a crescendo of gongs, cymbals, and other diabolical Chinese instruments, announces the arrival of the dragons, — red and green beasts twenty metres long. In some way or other they are lighted from within, which by night gives them an incandescent appearance; above the heads of the crowds they twist and undulate like the sulphurescent serpents in a Buddhist hell. The entire scene reflected in the water — the outline of palace and pagoda with their multiple roofs — is emphasized by lines of red lights that shine brightly this moonless and cloudy night.

When the big serpents have gone past, the Marble Bridge continues to pour at our feet a stream of humanity, although an irregular one, which moves tumultuously along with a formidable noise. It is the rest of our troops, the free soldiers following the procession with lanterns, also singing the "Marseillaise," or the "Sambre-et-Meuse," at the top of their lungs. Along with them are German soldiers arm-in-arm with them, increasing the volume of sound by adding their voices to the others, and singing with all their might the old French songs.

Midnight. The myriads of little red lanterns on the cornices of the old palace and pagodas have burned themselves out. Obscurity and the usual silence have come back to the lake and to the imperial woods. The Chinese princes have discreetly withdrawn, followed by their silk-robed attendants, and have been borne far away in their palanquins to their own dwellings in another part of the shadowy city.

It is now time for the cotillon, after a ball that was necessarily short, — a ball that seemed an impossibility, for there were scarcely a dozen dancing women, even including a pretty little twelve-year-old girl and her governess, to five hundred dancing men. It took place in the beautiful gilt pagoda, converted for the night into a ball-room; the dancers occupied the centre of the great empty space beneath the downcast gaze of the big alabaster goddess in the golden robes, who was my companion of last summer in the solitude of this same palace, together with a certain yellow and white cat. Poor goddess! A bed of natural iris has been arranged for the evening at her feet, and the injured background of her altar draped in blue satin, against the magnificent folds of which her figure stands out in ideal whiteness; her golden dress, embroidered with sparkling stones, shows to great advantage.

In spite of all effort to light this sanctuary and to decorate it with lanterns in the form of flowers and birds, it is too freakish a place for a ballroom. It is impossible to light up the corners and the gilded arches of the ceiling, and the presiding goddess is so mysteriously pale as to be embarrassing with that smile of hers, which seems to pity the puerility of our Occidental hopping and skipping; her eyes are downcast, that she may not see. This feeling of embarrassment is not peculiar to myself, for the young woman who is leading the cotillon, seized by some sudden fancy, leaves the room, taking with her the tambourine she is using in the figure that has just begun, and is followed by both dancers and onlookers, so that the temple is emptied, and our poor little cotillon, languidly continued for a time in the open air, comes to an end under the cedars of the esplanade, where a few lanterns are still burning.

One o'clock in the morning. Most of the guests have departed, having far to go in the darkness before reaching their dwellings. A few of the particularly faithful among the "Allies" remain, it is true, around the buffet where the champagne continues to flow, and the toasts to France grow warmer and warmer.

I was about to go off alone to my own palace, not far away, and was, in fact, already on the inclined plane leading to the Lake of the Lotus, when some one called out: "Wait for me; it will rest me to go along with you."

It was Colonel Marchand, and we walked along together over the Marble Bridge. The great winding sheet of silence and of night has fallen upon the Imperial City that had been filled for a single evening with music and light.

"Well," he questioned, "how did it go? what was your impression of it all?" And I replied as I felt, — that it was magnificently unusual, in a setting absolutely unparalleled.

Yet my friend Marchand seems rather depressed, and we scarcely speak, except for the occasional word that suffices between friends. There was, for one thing, the feeling of melancholy that comes from the fading away into the past of an event — futile though it was — which had brought us a few days' distraction from the preoccupations of life; and more than all this, there was another feeling, common to us both, which we understood almost without words as our heels clicked on the marble pavement in the silence that from moment to moment grew more solemn. It seemed to us that this evening had commemorated in a way the irremediable downfall of Pekin, or rather the downfall of a people. Whatever happens now, even though the remarkable Asiatic court comes back here, which seems improbable, Pekin is over, its prestige gone, its mysteries are open to the light of day.

Yet this Imperial City was one of the last refuges on earth of the marvellous and the unknown, one of the last bulwarks of a humanity so old as to be incomprehensible — nay, almost fabulous — to men of our times.

About the Author

Pierre Loti, one of the world's most prolific, romantic and exotic travel writers and novelists, was born as Julien Marie Viaud in Rochefort, western France in 1850, and wrote books while servicing as an officer in the French navy. His accounts of his time in China, from September 1900 to may 1901, were first published in the newspaper Le Figaro and were later published as Les Derniers Jours de Pekin in 1902. Loti died in 1923.